HOPE VERDAD PRESENTS
# THE BENCH
*A Parable About Life, Death, and Beyond*

FRANCESCA FLOOD ED.D.

Hope Verdad's The Bench

A Parable About Life, Death, and Beyond

Francesca Flood, Ed.D.

© 2024 Francesca Flood, All Rights Reserved

This is a work of fiction. Names, characters, places, and incidents are products of the author's imagination or used fictitiously. Any resemblance to actual events, locales, or persons, living or dead, is entirely coincidental.

No part of this book may be reproduced in any form or by any electronic or mechanical means, including information storage and retrieval systems, without permission in writing from the publisher, except by reviewers, who may quote short excerpts in a review or for quoting in appropriate articles.

Cover Photo—Will Paterson - Unsplash

Francesca@HopeVerdad.com

Visit www.HopeVerdad.com

Published by

Hope Verdad LLC

PO Box 364 Nellysford, VA 22958 USA

# Table of Contents

PREFACE..................................................................................1

CHAPTER ONE
KIP............................................................................................5

CHAPTER TWO
CARMEN.................................................................................13

CHAPTER THREE
LIAM.......................................................................................27

CHAPTER FOUR
JOSEPH...................................................................................51

CHAPTER FIVE
COTTON..................................................................81

CHAPTER SIX
KIP........................................................................109

ACKNOWLEDGMENTS..........................................125

Dedicated to

*Troy*

Whose short and challenging life taught us about love, grace, courage, and faith.

In a world where AI is becoming prolific

A human wrote this novella.

# Preface

From start to finish, the stories and messages in this novella came to me in a series of dreams. Night after night, vivid imagery introduced me to the five characters and their narrative. While I had confidence that I tapped into something (or something tapped into me), I hesitated to write it. Self-doubt slithers in like a reptile. Who was I to write on such a topic? Religion and faith are the stuff nations, and people go to war over.

Whenever I pushed the idea aside, a driving, insistent force said, "Write!" I felt a particular obligation to comply. These parables wanted to be born. When I hit a wall or struggled with a question far beyond my abilities, I assumed the writing ended. But the answers always came in a dream.

The Bench is a metaphor for life's struggles, unfairness, suffering, loss, and other calamities. No one goes through life unscathed; we all have at least one *Bench* moment. But what if we could talk to the one *person* we need the most to find comfort and closure or help us process an unanswerable question?

This writing is not theological, scholarly, or based on any faith tradition. Some religious and metaphysical terms are used merely as points of reference. I did not write this book to proselytize, convert, or diminish anyone's beliefs or faith traditions. It is written for consideration, perhaps as a guide, teacher, or to plant a seed of contemplation. A moment of grace—or just suppose.

We all have ideas about the meaning of life, what happens when we die, why we are here, and an entire litany of questions. Whether you subscribe to a religion or view yourself as a spiritual, agnostic, atheist, or some variation, this book asks you to keep an open mind.

Humans are a complex species from a physical or scientific perspective and a spiritual one. People struggle to find meaning, purpose, and contribution as they progress. We construct our own realities, ideologies, and social norms. Sometimes, we will die for or kill to defend them.

Many things divide us, including our fleshy container. Still, we can all agree upon a few absolute truths.

We are born. We will die. And between those two points, we will live; if blessed, we will love and be loved. Humans need to matter—if only to one person and belong to something greater.

My greatest wish as you encounter a Bench moment is that you are embraced by peace and assurance. On this magnificent journey called life, may you find purpose and know within your soul you are here because you matter.

# Chapter One
# Kip

Death circles his wife's bed like a bird of prey. Her death rattle fills every inch of the room. Kip Homestead holds her hand as tight as she can stand it. Somewhat loose. As he clasps it, he hopes some part of her will not be released from the mere 80 pound-sack that was once her body.

He wipes away a stealthy tear that slid from his eye and ran down his cheek. Kip offered so many of them as silent but unanswered prayers. No miracle will sweep in from the wings.

When her eyes closed, his breath caught. *Oh God.* Leaning over her, Kip places a finger under her nose. *Is she still breathing?* Her eyes open, startling him to jerk back.

"Sorry." Her voice is paper-dry and thin. And as if sorrow choreographed dancers, a tear drops.

"No. No." He rushes, brushing a strand of hair away from her face. "I thought you…." The final, unspeakable word lodges in his throat like a fist.

Her now oversized head, too big for the birdlike form, gives a slight side-to-side pull. Words require an energy that Lara Homestead no longer possesses. Her bony hand tries to grip his tighter. "I love you, Kip."

She is wheezing now, sucking and gulping for air that will not fill her lungs. The room becomes tomb silent. Days before, the medical team removed the monitoring equipment, the cannula, and every other measure to prolong her life.

*Her life.* Kip cringes at the irony of the word. Over the cancerous course of two years, pieces of his wife's life had been surgically cut off. Though his heart is cleaved in two, he understands what she needs to hear. "It's okay to let go, Lara. Fred and Crane are waiting at the rainbow bridge." He smiles at the thought of their two adopted border collies. "I love you."

The room's temperature drops. The warmth of Lara's energy and life force is gone. He folds her hands together as if in prayer and kisses her lips. In a day or two, they will give him her ashes to scatter into the wind. No gravesite, no service, and no announcements. Their burial plots, like everything else, were sold off. Nothing is left with bank accounts drained, and their home and cars repossessed. Caring for Lara's illness was a luxury that sucked away any remaining financial, family, and employment resources. Well-intentioned people on the periphery of disaster cannot sustain sympathy for protracted periods. Even Kip's job, though understanding for the first three months, filled his seat with another.

As he leaves the hospital, the wind whips paper and other debris around Kip. He glances across the parking lot and walks toward a dumpster where he hid the remnants of their lives in a shopping cart. Any observing stranger might think it's filled with junk - papers, photos, and worn clothes. To Kip, these are his last treasures.

He zips his well-used coat and turns up the collar. Ominous clouds march across the sky, threatening to attack. As Kip pushes his cart forward, he wonders if the shelters will have beds tonight. When nasty weather arrives, they seldom do. Though he focuses straight ahead, passing pedestrians give him a wide berth with downcast eyes. Kip has become one of the countless, scorned, and shunned homeless, whose 'invisible' presence is vast.

*Yeah, I know.* He thinks, looking at the people. *I thought it only happened to the other guy, too. But it's only one catastrophe away.*

The chilly wind stings his face and whips his stringy, oily hair. Once a clean-shaven face, Kip's beard is now crusted with bits of ice and the residue of crackers from the hospital's vending machine. *God, am I a cliché?* He struggles to place one tattered sneaker before the other. I can join Lara. At 40, Kip still cannot understand how their lives turned out.

As rain and ice pelt his eyes, he blinked, pushing the cart forward. *Grateful for no kids.* Though at one point, they weren't thankful. Lara and Kip Homestead would have loved having children. *I would've loved to have more time.*

As he enters a park, a sharp pain radiates from his chest, down his arms, and squeezes like a vise around his back. Panting, his consciousness dims. He needs a place to land. His feet move as if attached to bricks. Huffing, he throws himself onto a metal bench covered in an icy sheen. His heart throbs as he places his hands on his thighs and dips his head.

The keening sound is supernatural; for a moment, Kip tries to identify its owner. His insides and soul are unmooring as if trying to escape the horror and the unimaginable grief. "Why?" His scream is so anguished that any remaining birds take flight. He screams again, "Why? What did Lara or I ever do to deserve this?" He bows his head as the sobbing continues to wrack his body. The snot from his nose freezes as he attempts to wipe it away. "If you're there… listening… please."

The bitter cold seeps into his bones. Freezing to death has appeal. *It might be a blessing.* A hand touches him with a pulsating warmth that flows through Kip's body. Fingers cup around his shoulder, forcing an exhalation that empties his lungs, sweeping away the weight of grief and despair. The stabbing pain in his chest ceases.

As Kip twists toward this stranger, he raises his hand to block a light. When his eyes adjust, he studies the stranger's face. His skin is a rich, olive complexion with a thick, dark, and full beard. Shoulder-length, wiry hair frames his face. Kip assesses the man's clothing, rubs his eyes, and looks again.

The man is wearing nothing more than a burlap tunic with long sleeves. Cinched around his waist is a knotted cord. A purple sash drapes across his chest. Kip smiles, thinking it reminds him of his Boy Scout days without badges. He glances at the man's feet and is stunned by nothing more than a pair of black shower slippers.

Using the heel of his hands, Kip blinks harder this time, trying to rub away the hallucination. But when he opens his eyes, the stranger is still present, resting his hand on Kip.

"Who are you?" Kip asks.

The man turns to face Kip. "I am - who you need me to be."

"But I…. I might know you from somewhere," Kip stammers. Inside the cobwebbed corners of his brain, he searches for the connection. *I know him.* He hears faint snippets of songs. His mother's hand. His eyes widen as he sucks in a breath. "Are you…?"

Keeping his hand on Kip's shoulder, the stranger leans in closer. "I am - who you need me to be." He repeats.

Their eyes meet. Every cell within Kip awakens to love, compassion, and peace as if pulled into the ocean's undertow. Whatever gift this man possesses, Kip does not want to return to life's present shore.

The man closes his eyes, breaking the connection.

Kip's hands are pink with warmth. Desolation and hopelessness fade. He continues to study his hands, hoping they will encourage and strengthen his next question. Looking up, he stares into the man's face. "Why?"

The visitor cups his hand around Kip's ear, leans in, and whispers.

# Chapter Two
# Carmen

The aroma of spent wax, lemon oil, and smoke spirals to the cathedral ceiling. Carmen Angelica Lopez de Santiago folds a ten-dollar bill. She pushes it into the offering slot on the metal stand holding several votive candle rows. Almost every candle is lit, most of them by her. It is one of the many rituals that she remembers from her childhood. Lighting candles and whispering prayers for dead loved ones or for special intentions, like the sick people she cares for every day at work.

Just like her mother and mother's mother and a long line of Lopez women, she believes in the feminine power of God's mother—Mary. *Women bear children and are the counterbalance needed in a patriarchal world.* She blesses herself.

This devotional candle stand is more ornate, with metal flowers and leaves woven throughout its framework. It rests before a six-foot statue of Mary—or, in the Mexican tradition, Our Lady of Guadalupe. Carmen inventories the adjoining shimmering wicks, wondering what other worshippers have prayed for. *Are any of them offered in thanks for answered prayers?* She reaches for the long, thin stick to light a new candle. A neighboring candle extinguishes as her stick catches flame, creating a puff of smoke that assaults her nostrils.

The scent traveling to Carmen's brain triggers her. Her palms sweat. The pounding of rushing blood enters her ears. Her legs wobble as she grabs the stand, hoping she does not pull it over. She squeezes her eyes to shut out the scene replaying in her mind. Carmen tries to inhale through her mouth, not wanting to remember that metallic odor of blood. Blood and flesh and bits of bone that cling to the walls and bedcovers. The acrid stench of gunpowder. The dim room where her fifteen-year-old son Thomas blew his brains out. Her sweet boy with life's road stretched out before him was now gone.

Carmen inhales through her mouth. Breathing deep

into her diaphragm as the psychiatrist taught her. *In*. She inhales. *Out*. She exhales a huge breath. Trembling, she grips the wooden pew and makes her way to sit. *Shh*, she tells her heart to be quiet as it pumps like she is sprinting. Perhaps she is running, wanting to race through this life. However, Carmen believes this is a sin. God gives you life. We cannot take or wish it away. She thinks of Thomas' immortal soul and pulls down the padded kneeler.

Holding an ancient set of wooden rosary beads, she blesses herself and kisses the cross. She begins her prayer in Spanish. "Holy Mary, Mother of God, pray for us sinners," she whispers to the Blessed Mother statue before her. Carmen believes that if anyone can understand her anguish, her crushed spirit, Mary would—the Mother of Jesus, who lost her child to crucifixion. The word pecadores, "sinners," catches in her throat, and she brushes away a tear. Her beautiful child, Thomas. The boy with a smile as bright as the sun. Who hugged her as if it was the end of the world. And it was—for her loving son.

Having taken his own life, Carmen ruminates on the possibility that Thomas's eternal soul would not enter heaven. *Suicide is a mortal and unforgivable sin*. She remembered the teachings from her early catechism. Yet the mother hopes God and the Catholic Church have softened their stance. *People commit worse sins and deserve hell. Not a child who didn't harm anyone but himself.*

She remembers another teenage boy who committed suicide five years prior. During the boy's funeral Mass, the presiding priest called the deceased a sinner, condemning the child and suggesting heaven was out of reach. Horrified, the parents reported the incident, and the Archdiocese of Detroit soon apologized, tempering the position on suicide and assuring that the priest would not preside over funerals until tutored.

"Now and at the hour of our death. Amen," Carmen finishes her prayer and blesses herself. Her heart calms. *Oh, holy Mother. How did you go on after losing your child?* She searches the sorrowful face of the plaster statue, hoping for an answer.

Pushing open the arched wooden door adorned with wrought iron, Carmen steps outside into the sunlight. The buds of defiant new leaves cling to the trees as if announcing they have survived the winter. Spring arrived. Yet Carmen believes her life will now be an eternal winter. Cold, dark, and without promise. She shivers at the thought of losing her faith. Even Mother Teresa experienced the dark night of the soul—a time when everything was hollow and without purpose.

Her husband, Tom Santiago, has been a pillar of strength for her and their two younger boys. He has had his moments, but the stoicism of his childhood teaching has kicked in. He comforts and assures them. The younger boys need to believe their father's promises. Although Tom tries to inflate her outlook, she collapses, like the lawn decorations seen at Christmas.

Carmen's mind runs through a labyrinth of questioning scenarios. *If only. What if? Why? What did I miss? How did I let this happen?* Everything seemed fine. Until it horrifically wasn't. The family therapist suggested they sell the house and begin a fresh start. They did. Tom and the younger children emerge from a chrysalis of doom—or, as Carmen thinks, a death shroud. She cannot emerge from her glass coffin. Life is moving on. A huge part, if not all, died with Thomas.

Entering the park, the high-pitched giggling pricks her ears. Carmen watches the youngsters in bright-colored sweaters running around the trees in a game of chase. A woman clutches her infant swaddled in a wool blanket while her foot rocks a stroller with a sleeping toddler. A boy, perhaps seven or eight, walks past her. His corn silk blond hair shimmers with the sunlight. Carmen catches his gray-blue eyes and his profound sense of sadness. She wonders how she recognizes this grief in a stranger and yet missed it in her child. High up, Carmen spies a bird building her nest while squirrels scamper back and forth with their loot. Everywhere she turns is life—except one.

A man throwing bread to pigeons stands, crumples his empty bag, and tosses it in a trash can. Carmen wants to sit to catch her breath and collect herself before returning home. Her sons need her. So did Thomas. *And I failed you.* She fears a dam of endless sobs will reopen but refuses to give in, seeing this as another failure.

Carmen sits on a bench, gazing at the sun. A welcoming, warm breeze flows past her. A familiar scent lingers. "Thomas?" Her voice borders on giddiness. Others have told her that a deceased loved one sends signs- a cardinal, butterfly, favorite song, or scent. She brings her hands to her heart. *Thomas, I miss you so much.* Her eyes closed. Some inexplicable force squeezed the air from her lungs.

"Hello." His dark-brown hair is still shaggy and dips into his eyes. He swipes the strand across his forehead. His mouth pulls into a smile, exposing an endearing snaggletooth.

"Thomas?" Her eyes open, exposing the sclera. Her mind knows the voice is off. Her heart aches to believe. Carmen's body convulses, rocking back and forth as if possessed. "Thomas? Thomas?" She blinks, trying to signal her brain. Her heart wins. "My boy! My baby!" Her pitch is so high that the words screech. She falls into her son's chest. "Madre de Dios," she sobs, reaching for her son. His skin is translucent, unable to contain the light within him.

A few feet from the bench, another young mother is alarmed by the woman speaking to no one and gesticulating. She gives the woman more expansive space and ushers her child past.

Thomas wraps his arms around the mother's wracking body. "Shush—it's okay." His tone is soothing. His hand strokes her back. "It's okay," he consoles.

Carmen raises her head and stares into her son's hazel eyes. "Oh, Thomas, I've missed you so much, my son." She is so relieved that the thought of how he appeared never enters her mind. Carmen believes in miracles, and this is unquestioningly one.

The pair sit for a few moments, embracing the rhythm of their joined hearts. A gentle breeze flows past them, and Thomas moves his mother to an arm's length position. "Everything is okay." He assures.

She studies his face, wanting to burn the memory

of it in her mind. "How are you… Why did you… Where are you…?" The questions spill from her mouth. Carmen wants to comprehend. Needs answers. A terror that he will vanish again before she understands grips her. To reassure herself that the whole Thomas — her flesh and blood—is sitting beside her, she holds his hand, squeezing so tight the blood drains from his fingertips.

Thomas's voice is almost inaudible. He whispers to himself, "Sorry." His eyes moisten. "It's an inadequate word. When someone takes their life, they don't stop to think about the carnage they leave behind. We must love others, but we must also love ourselves." He shook his head. "It's hard to understand this when one suffers from soul-crushing torment, feels alone, or is confused. The consequences of taking one's life are not well thought out. A regrettable and misunderstood act." Thomas sits, allowing her to process his words.

"Are you…Are you in heaven, Thomas?" She twists the wedding band on her finger, now wishing she hadn't asked the question. She is terrified he will talk about sin and hell.

Thomas cocks his head as if confused by the question. Carmen is about to fill the silence when he responds, "Humans and religions create heaven, adding unique embellishments. Heaven is not somewhere up there." He points his index finger upward and smiles. "Heaven is the universe and all within it. Our soul, our life force, returns to the One Collective Source. Some call this God. The universal truth - God is love."

His lips are moving, but Carmen is unsure if she understands what he is saying. "Heaven is where we'll all meet again." A belief so embedded that she needs Thomas's assurance.

"You will meet again, but not as an individual with a mortal body. The human form is temporary. It dies, and the soul returns. Bodies are not needed for recognition. The Sanskrit word 'namaste' is the essence of souls recognizing souls."

"Wait. I'm not following," Carmen replies.

"Human birth and death are like the cycle of rain. Water evaporates from the oceans, rising from the surface to form clouds. Individual droplets of rain fall to earth, but they return to the total collection."

"So, we don't return to heaven as humans?" She asks, bewildered.

"God isn't human. Not a white man with a long, flowing beard. Nothing like the statutes and paintings."

Thomas chuckles and shakes his head at the notion. "Humanity is created in the Creator's image, but humans try to create God in theirs. Humans are a particle of God that will return to the Source, like metal shavings to a magnet."

Carmen's mouth pinches. *What is he saying?* "Wait. We reunite with our loved ones after we die, right?" Her tone becomes more insistent and desperate. "We live a righteous life, and we go to heaven. Those who have unforgiven sins go to hell." She draws her hand to her mouth in horror. *Thomas died in sin.*

"God doesn't keep score. Love isn't concerned with doling out punishment. That's a well-developed human skill. Humans need hell to mete out their sense of justice. If people don't get the punishment they deserve while alive—well, fire and brimstone, they will when they die." He mocks in a deeper tone. "Life has to be fair, right? Even if it happens in death." Thomas bends over and plucks a blade of new grass that worked through the soil. An ear-to-ear grin spreads across his face as he places it on his tongue, moves the blade under his nose, and inhales. "As sentient beings, humans have the gift of tangible experience." He inhales the grass again. "Such a gift." He closes his eyes and exhales with an expression of complete satisfaction.

Volcanic angst bubbles inside her. He is dismantling her beliefs. *Yes! I want people who commit evil acts to burn in hell. But…I want Thomas exempted from these rules—a* deep crevice forms between her eyebrows.

"Ah, another human condition." He twirls the blade of grass between his fingers. "Judgment and societal norms can be tricky. Who makes the rules? Who is exempt from the rules and decides what is an adequate reward or punishment?"

"Well, if we don't have to worry about punishment, why not just live in complete sinfulness?" She huffs.

"Because humans are not born in sin or to commit sin."

Carmen recognizes her son's face, eyes, and the tiny white scar he gained as a toddler at his temple. However, this son is wiser and more eloquent. Her Thomas was shy, prone to awkwardness, and sometimes couldn't finish a sentence. This boy is kind, but something is off about him. *Is this Thomas? A specter sent as a gift, a second chance? Or something else?* "Thomas, you know how much we loved…love you, right?" A lump lodges in her throat.

"A mother's love is quite close to agape love. They are closer to the Divine as creators. They speak to God through prayer for their children." He reaches for her hand. Her anxiety calms when he touches her skin. "Agape love transcends everything and persists without conditions."

Her eyes shimmer with tears. "I guess losing you is the price of our failures. Why Thomas? Why?" Carmen uses the back of her hand to wipe streaming tears.

"His death was not your failure. People lose their footing on the journey. They lose hope or feel alone. Some use suicide to escape the torment of bullying or other suffering. A misguided choice."

"Choice?" Carmen hisses the word and recoils her hand from his. "Choice!" she repeats. "Choice is picking out your clothes or food or… it's not about suicide."

Thomas closes his eyes, and when he reopens them, Carmen reads a profound sadness that tightens in her chest.

"Choice is free will," he murmurs. "Human agency that separates from the Divine. Free will often turns into pride without care. An addictive and seductive sense of omnipotence will make you believe in this illusory world." The light seeps from his pores as if sweating, creating a nimbus around his form.

"Illusory?" Her mouth forms a line of skepticism.

"The only permanence in human existence is love. It transcends death. Your son died, yet your love for him continues." He shrugs and smiles. "Everything else"—he waves his hands in a fluid motion— "is a temporal illusion that fades. What is that saying?" He rests a finger across his chin as if to ponder the answer. "U-Haul trucks don't follow hearses." He chuckles and stops when he catches her face.

The young man reaches for her hand.

Carmen swallows hard. "You're not my Thomas. Are you?" Her words are not accusatory but resigned. "He wouldn't talk like this." She searches his face. He is disappearing into the sun's brilliance. "Who are you?"

"I am - who you need me to be."

"Is Thomas okay?" she whispers.

He embraces Carmen into the light. She gasps as a rip releases her soul from her body. Like paper in a flame, layers of beliefs and teachings curl away. She is floating, drawn toward a pulsating light. Once in its radiance, Carmen weeps, overcome with intense love. Her love combines with all love from the past, present, and future in this place. It is so overwhelming that her conscious mind is almost shattered.

* * *

The remnants of winter leaves scrape along the path as a cool breeze blows. Carmen sits on the bench and stares at the setting sun. The ghost of Thomas, whoever or whatever he was, has disappeared. The incredible sensation of love she experienced remains. She hopes it will last forever. This is the connection to her son, his eternal presence.

The weight and suffocation of her grief are lifted. Knowing her son is in this indescribable place gives her peace. *Can I share this with Tom? The boys?* Can she explain it? Would they believe her? But for having the experience herself, would she?

Walking down the path that leaves the park, Carmen's tranquil state churns with questions. She wishes she had asked more. *Am I following the right faith? Is reincarnation possible? Are there other worlds?* These are questions for the mind, not the heart. She does not need these answers. Carmen understands the rare gift. A glimpse of the universal truth: God is Love.

# CHAPTER THREE
# LIAM

Liam freezes, hearing the four-note doorbell. His heart is pounding, and a wave of nausea roils his stomach. "If I hide, it can't find me." He drops to the floor and crawls under the bed, pulling his Buzz Lightyear comforter to conceal his hiding place. At seven, the boy understands pain.

The bell rings again. The muffled sounds of voices waft up the stairs to his room. Liam cannot make out the words. He doesn't want to and chews on a cuticle until it bleeds. He wants to suck this thumb. *It'd upset Mom, though.* Liam knows his mother has had a lifetime of upset.

The door closes, and the sound of muted footsteps climbing the steps causes him to shiver. *Please.* Liam's sweaty hands clasped together. His mouth is dry. The doorbell is the Grim Reaper in disguise. *Please. Please.* His stomach groans as he tries to burrow further under the bed, cowering against the wall.

"Liam?" His mother, Prudence, pokes her head into his room. "Liam?" she calls again, peeking below. "Hi, honey." Her face is angelic. A safe harbor that shields him. Liam shuffles his feet, pushes off, and crawls towards her. His mother lifts him and squeezes him close to her. He inhales, taking in her scent. "Hey, Champ," her voice coos as if in song. "Don't be frightened."

The young mother combs her fingers through his corn silk blond hair and puts him on the bed. "It was the mailman with a package." She places her hand under his chin, causing him to see sincerity in her eyes. His gray-blue eyes are wide, filled with fear. Her heart breaks. It has become a familiar scene. "Oh, Liam." She says, clutching him as if he, too, might vanish.

In his mother's arms, the night their world ended comes rushing back.

\* \* \*

The sky had cracked open with a deluge of rain. What

seemed like buckets of water pounded against the asphalt, raising oil patches. The doorbell sounded while Liam and his mother were preparing dinner. "I'll get it!" He yelled, jumping up and down and scampering toward the door.

"Hang on," his mother laughed, pushing aside the cutting board of chopped vegetables. Before she could catch him, a nearly seven-year-old Liam was at the door, twisting the knob and pulling the door open.

A giant loomed in the doorway. A crescent moon half hidden by clouds seemed to rest on his massive shoulder. He was wearing the brightest neon-yellow jacket Liam had ever seen. His baseball cap had the word POLICE embroidered across the front panel. It was ineffective against the teeming rain as drops slid down the man's thick neck. "Is your mother home?" His voice was a deep baritone with no hint of a smile.

Liam stared, mouth gaping.

A second police officer stood behind the giant. She was shorter, squat, and just as somber.

"May we step inside?" the hulking man asked.

Liam nodded, still gawking.

The police officers stepped into the house. The first

officer bent at the waist and asked again. "Is your mother home?"

Liam's lips glued together.

His mother entered the hallway. "Can I help you?"

"Ma'am." He touched the bill of the cap and studied his shoes. The second officer's eyes fixed on the wall, eschewing the moment. A puddle of water collected around their feet.

Liam wondered if his mom would be angry with them, knowing how often he had been told to remove his muddy sneakers.

"Can I help you, officers?" Prudence asked once more. Her face, though calm, was now a shade of gray—a tremor in her hand.

"Ma'am." The policeman's tone softened. The corners of his lips turned down. "I'm Officer Santos, and this is Officer Boxley. Are you related to Phillip English?"

"Yes, he's my husband." Her lips trembled as she placed a hand on her mouth. "What's happened?" She moved closer to the policeman, grabbing hold of Liam on the way.

The policewoman checked her partner and asked, "Would it be all right if your son and I go to his room?"

Prudence's eyes darted from the two officers to her child. "Liam?" Her breath labored.

"No," Liam wailed. "I want to stay with you, Mom."

"It's okay," Prudence said, without knowing the lingering effect of the moment.

The policeman removed his baseball cap. "We have bad news. Your husband was killed in a car crash this evening."

Prudence crumpled to the floor like a marionette whose string had been cut.

"Mom!" Liam cried, rushing to his mother.

The policeman was quick, catching her head before it made contact. Holding the woman under her arms, he helped her sit on the couch. He entered the kitchen, found a glass, and filled it with water.

Liam was stock-still as the horror unfolded in slow motion.

As Prudence sipped, a wave of nausea rose. Though she tried to stifle her sobs, the mournful sound seeped through the walls. "What happened?" Her eyes were already bloodshot.

"Someone ran a stop sign and T-boned your husband's vehicle. The rain, visibility…" His voice trailed off. "The impact of the truck killed your husband. I'm sorry, ma'am."

Although the officer was polite and comforting, his dialog became buzzing. While the second officer explained the procedures, Prudence's mind had gone to Phillip. Realizing that he would never walk through their front door and into their lives again terrified her.

The heavens mourned the day of Phillip English's funeral with a torrential downpour. Attendees dressed in black were dutifully sympathetic. But as they left the cemetery and headed to their cars, they would return to normalcy. For the mother and son, life would not be so kind.

When Liam returned to his second-grade class, students shied away from him as if losing one's father was contagious. Shyness morphed into cruelty children often displayed at any sign of difference. "Who's gonna come on Father's Day, Liam?" Charlie, a plump, unpopular boy, taunted him. Charlie's meanness increased, goaded by student onlookers.

Mindy Williams always liked Liam. Despite the taunting of their classmates, she held steady to him. As the child of a single mother, she was also cast as a misfit with her tangled hair, oversized glasses, and worn clothing. "He'll get his. Mean gets repaid," she said with such an air of certainty that Liam almost believed her. "Karma is real." She continued.

"What's karma?" he asked one afternoon as the pair sat isolated on the school playground.

"It's when you get payback for being good. Or being bad." The glass lenses magnified her eyes, giving her face a bug-like appearance. "You might think you're getting away with something, but you're not. The Man upstairs is in charge." She pointed upward.

"God?" he asked, furrowing his eyebrows.

Mindy raised her shoulders to her ears. "I guess so."

Liam's face flushed a deep pink. "I don't believe in Him."

"How come?" Her tone was more curious than correcting.

"Cause a god wouldn't have gotten my dad killed. Why'd my dad get karma?" His sarcasm was not missed.

"Oh," she whispered, looking down at her friend's hand and taking it. "What's your mom say about that?"

He wiped his eyes. "She might not believe in Him either."

Three weeks after their discussion, Liam accepted the veracity of Mindy's karma theory. Charlie arrived at school distraught and disheveled. His pants were wrinkled from waist to foot. His hair was unclean and matted to his head. Liam wondered if the boy had lost weight as he appeared gaunter.

"What's wrong with Charlie?" Liam asked Mindy as they walked through the hall adorned with student art.

"His mom abandoned him and his dad," she said, adjusting her glasses. "Just left and didn't come home. Only a note. Said she was done."

They smiled and said in unison, "Karma."

* * *

Liam is changing. Once an energetic child with an insatiable curiosity, he has crawled into a shell. An emotionless mask replaced his infectious smile. Prudence's son is sliding into depression if he hasn't already arrived. Now quick to anger, a meanness reverberates in a boy who cried when a butterfly died.

"And you're sure Liam will be safe, Bill?" She asks the Little League coach. The mother wants every reassurance, with no father to protect her child.

"Prudence. Little League is what Liam needs. He's outside, interacting with other kids, and it will give him something else to focus on," the coach assures her.

"Okay, I'll take him to the park on Saturday. Thanks, Bill." She signed off, hoping she was doing the right thing. Liam has become clingy, needy, and afraid of his shadow. Prudence wonders if she should take him to the sports store to help purchase the things he will need for Little League. Then she thinks better of it because he argues about everything.

Liam climbs into his car seat. His face puckers into a scowl. "Why do I have to sit in this baby chair?" he huffs as Prudence tightens the belts.

"Until you're eight, it's the law." She stops short of a snarky reply. Her patience is frayed, too.

Liam whined all morning about wearing a uniform and missing his cartoons. He complained about chocolate chip pancakes—his favorite. Prudence hopes today will be a turning point. It has been six months since Phillip died. "I miss him too, Champ." She reaches for the tissue box and dabs her eyes.

Liam examines his mother's face in the rearview mirror. New creases on her forehead and between her brows emerged. Her lips never curl up at the end anymore. The heaviness of the father's death drapes over them.

The boy sits still and stares out the window. When they arrive at the ballpark, Liam unbuckles himself. Prudence opened the door, and Liam stepped out of the car into the blinding sun.

Kids in white uniforms with blue numbers stitched on their backs run around the field. Coach Bill Mitchell approaches them. "Hey, Liam. Prudence." He shakes the mother's hand. "Welcome to the team, Liam. Why don't you join the others in the warm-up?"

Liam moves towards the other children and glances over his shoulder. He wants some sign from his mother.

Prudence smiles and waves a hand to go ahead. "His father just started playing catch with him before the accident." She bows her head and sniffs. "He's not as far along as the other kids."

"Everyone starts somewhere, Prudence. He'll be

fine." Coach Mitchell assures her. "The parents are sitting in the bleachers if you want to join them. Let's start."

The shrill whistle catches everyone's attention. The boys form two lines to play a practice game. The coach assigns Liam to the group first. Confidence radiates off the other children, who appear bigger than him. He waits, third in line. The first boy struck out. The second hit a line drive and ran.

"Okay, Liam," Coach Mitchell encourages, "Play ball."

Liam's palms are damp with sweat. He rubs his hands on his uniform pants, takes the bat, and thinks about his father's advice. *What did Dad say about not choking up on it?* The sun burns through his helmet as he tries to remember the time he and his father played.

"Strike one!" Coach Mitchell bellows. It startles Liam. The pitcher's face twists into a snarl. Liam is intimidated. He raises the bat, waits for the pitch, and swings.

"Strike two!" The voice yells.

Groans and snickers fill Liam's ears. His muscles tense.

"Hey, Champ. Don't grip that too high. Inhale, see the ball, connect with the ball, Phillip English encourages, whispering in his son's ear.

Sitting in the bleachers, parents hear the crisp, single-note *ping* as the bat connects. Eyes follow as it sails over the pitcher's head and, despite their best efforts, the outfielders. Liam's pent-up rage and grief channel into the ball that soars past the players and beyond the park.

"Wow!" Coach Mitchell roars, encouraging Liam and the player before him to run the bases.

When the duo returned to home plate, the teammates enveloped them. Parents are whooping, jumping, and whistling. Coach Mitchell claps Liam on the back, and his teammates pump his hand.

Prudence weeps, watching a smile spread across her son's face.

Liam picks his mother out of the crowd. She is waving at him. He reads her lips as the word 'proud' is formed. For a fleeting moment, he remembers happiness instead of sorrow. *Thanks, Dad.*

Driving home, Prudence suggests, "I say we go for ice cream." She glances over her shoulder for his confirmation. Liam's grin vanished. "Champ?" A deep frown returned to her son's face. "Liam?"

He is sullen. "Dad should have been here today."

"I know, Liam. But he would have been proud of you." Prudence holds short. At one point, she would have assured her son that his father watched over him. But the widow will not share these platitudes. She is unsure that some divine entity is concerned with the minutia of individuals' lives.

The spell of celebration has vanished, and silence once again takes hold. When Prudence pulls the car into the garage, Liam asks, "Mom, can I go to the park for a while?"

Nowadays, Prudence insists on going with him. But her son needs time to process the emotions swirling inside his head.

"Okay, Liam." She hands him Phillip's phone. "Be home in a half hour. We'll have pizza tonight." Life's injustice weighs on her young son's shoulders.

Liam walks to the end of his block, where the park is across the street. Cars speed past him, ignoring the 'Slow. Children at Play' sign. Waiting for a break, he skips to the other side. Kids swing, crawl through tubes, and climb slides on the black rubber-matted playground. Caregivers chat, keeping one eye on their youngsters.

He steps down a path lined with pavers and finds a bench nestled under a tree with white blooms. As Liam sits, he catches a ladybug crawling along the seat. He picks it up and squeezes it with his thumb and index finger.

"Hey, Liam," Phillip English says. "Why do you want to do that?"

Liam drops the bug, which senses a reprieve and flies away. "Dad?" He raises a hand over his eyes to block the sunlight.

"I am—who you need me to be."

"Daddy!" Liam sighs, releasing all his breath.

"You're angry, Champ. But killing that insect or hurting anything else won't change things."

Though the child is stunned by his father's appearance, the admonition still stings as red creeps up the back of his neck. Liam burrows his face into his father's chest and cries. "Dad, why did you leave us?" He grips the man's waist and clings. Like breaking waves, sobs wrack the boy's body.

"Your dad didn't want to leave you, Liam. Or

your mom. But sometimes accidents happen. It's hard to understand that." He rubs the top of the boy's head and wraps his muscular arm around the child's slender shoulders.

"But why'd God choose you to have the accident?" he asks, forgetting he stopped believing in these things. "Why you?" Liam peers up at his father's face. A face he worries he would not recall if not for the pictures he and his mother share. The man's skin shimmers, reflecting more than sunlight. "Can you come back? Please, Dad. I need you. Mom needs you." Tears spilled from his eyes.

Phillip holds the son's face in his hands and brushes away a stray lock of blond hair. "No, Liam." Your dad can't come back. Sometimes, accidents happen with a nudge from humans. And sometimes things happen without understanding why."

"I don't understand," Liam says, rubbing his eyes.

"Humans make choices. They rarely grasp the ripple effect of their actions, like the man who slammed into the car. He glanced down at his phone because it rang- just a glance- but that is all it took."

"I hate him!" Liam squeezes his fists into balls and bares his teeth.

"And then what?" Phillip's eyes search the boy's face.

"Wha?" The boy pauses, dazed by the father's response.

"So, you hate him. And then what? When you can't hurt him, you take it out on the people and things you love and who love you. Like that bug or your mother." The man pulls Liam closer.

"Anger is normal, Liam. It isn't fair. But anger has a beginning and must also have an end. Otherwise, Liam, the boy, dies, and an angry stranger takes his place."

"I'm so mad." Liam thrusts out his lower lip. I want him to get karma!" he says, proud of his new weapon.

"Karma?" Phillip lifts the boy's chin. "Karma pretends life is a giant scale where all the good and all the bad balance out, Liam." He pauses. "People shouldn't do good deeds expecting payback. They should do good because it shows love and requires no compensation. Many times, people do bad things, and there is no karma. No payback."

"But that man took you away from me!" Liam shrieks. "I want him to have payback."

"Suppose you made a mistake that hurt someone? Would you want them to hate you forever or hope something bad happens to you?"

Liam shakes his head. "No, 'cause I didn't mean it."

"The guy who caused the accident didn't mean it, Liam. He made a costly mistake that he will live with for the rest of his life. Perhaps he will bring something positive from this," Phillip cradles the boy. "Do you understand?" His voice is just above a whisper.

Liam sobs. "But it isn't fair."

"Life isn't fair in this world, Liam. Life is an imperfect experience that doesn't ensure everyone gets treated equally. Some people have more than they need, and some have nothing." He readjusts the boy on his lap. "You remember seeing homeless people, right?"

"Yes." Liam is tentative now.

"Your cousin Kimberly uses a wheelchair. She did nothing wrong. Neither did her parents. People will become sick and die, even little kids—not because they did anything wrong, and bad things still happen. This place here," he says, pointing to the ground. "Doesn't mean humans live a happy life where only positive things happen."

"But why? If God loves us, why does he allow it to happen?"

"Humans are born to experience life- all of it, the good and the bad. If everything here were perfect, there would be no point in creation, and people wouldn't know the difference."

Liam squinted his eyes. "Yes, they would."

"How?" Phillip raised one corner of his mouth in a playful smirk.

Liam scratches his head. "They just would!" he says brazenly, folding his arms.

"It doesn't work that way, Champ. Think about it like this. You've been sad and angry, emotions that don't feel right. You understand these are bad feelings because you know what happiness feels like. It's like eating a lemon and then ice cream. You know about the taste of one because of the other.

"Opposites." Liam nods. "We learned about it in class."

"When someone dies, people think they will always be sad, or they *should* only be sad. When something wonderful happens, and there's joy, they feel guilty or ashamed." He dips his head, staring into the boy's eyes. "Like when you hit that home run today?"

"You saw that?" Liam's face beams.

The man nods his head. "It's all right to enjoy life, Liam."

"But why do we need bad things, Dad?"

"It's difficult to understand, even when you're older, Liam. But sometimes, humans learn a lot about themselves when bad things happen. You might see something is wrong and make it right instead of just watching. You didn't choose for the bad thing to happen but chose your response."

"Like helping Mom carry groceries, not just watching her."

"That's one example. When bad things happen, people want to know why. Their baby drowns, or they develop cancer, or lose a leg, or…"

"Their dad dies in an accident," Liam interjects.

"Yes. Humans have to make sense of tragedy so that it has meaning and is not random. They might ensure no other parent or person suffers the same misfortune."

Liam is pensive. "Like the moms who don't want people to drive after drinking."

"Correct!" the man smiles. They've lost a child and want to make sure other parents don't. Loss is never easy, Liam. But it can make you more aware of your blessings and more appreciative. Suffering can make the bliss sweeter."

"Why should I be thankful for losing you?"

"Liam. It's not that you should appreciate losing your dad. That would be wrong. But when you lose someone, you become more mindful of the people you have and treasure them more. But you should never, ever find joy in the suffering of others because those two things don't belong together."

"Like Charlie." Liam dips his head.

"Like Charlie," the man agrees. Being sad and angry is a bad feeling, even worse when you are alone. People avoid sad and angry people because they don't want to experience those emotions. Remember when Mindy stood by your side?"

"Yeah, Mindy's cool." Liam beams.

"Mindy remembers what it's like to be without

friends. You know what losing a parent is like, even if that parent didn't die."

"Like Charlie," Liam replies. "I know how he feels."

"Sometimes, Liam, the better person within, awakens when bad things happen. Charlie, like you, needs a friend. If every person practiced more kindness, this world would have far less sadness."

"I understand." A melancholy smile crosses Liam's face.

"You can learn from losing your father. You'll grow into a kinder person, recognizing the sadness in others. Terrible experiences build greater endurance. You will help people who are hurting. Like your mom. Can you see it?"

Liam remembers his mother's face in the rearview mirror. He is unclear about aging, but his mother seems older and wearier. "Yes."

"Your mom needs you, Liam. She's sad, too, and worries about you. Your father is gone, but you and your mother will find joy. You didn't die with your dad." Phillip takes Liam off his lap and plants him on the path—light ripples off the man's skin, casting an aura.

The man is vanishing. "I love you, Dad. Please don't go!" His chest is heaving as the figure fades.

"You will always love your father, Liam. That is the connection."

Rage snakes up, ready to strike. "No!" He shouts at the sky. NNo!" His voice falls to a whimper. Liam may not understand everything discussed, but his mom needs him. He is tired of being angry. *That won't bring back my dad.*

As he walks up the pavers to the path, Liam English thinks about the imperfection of this world. He considers his choices, allowing his rage to control his life. *If anger has a beginning, it must have an end.* He replays his father's words. *Why is anger so easy?*

He ducks under a dipping branch along the trail toward home. The word *choice* flutters through his mind. A man who glanced at his phone while driving. The mother who left Charlie. Children shunning Mindy. *Choices*. He thinks about his classmate Charlie, ashamed that he gloated at the boy's suffering. He promises to befriend him.

Liam checks both ways and crosses the street. Staring at his father's phone, he was gone for twenty-five minutes. The boy picks up his pace, knowing his tardiness will worry his mother. A little girl who lives on his block walks past him. Her hand brushes against his leg. He studies the younger child and notices her sneakers and sweater are soiled. Unkempt hair frames a tear-streaked face. She's running her hand along a white picket fence that has fallen into disrepair. His heart aches.

"Hey." He gives her a shy smile. "Are you okay?"

The girl shrugs as if unsure of her circumstances. Piles of unfurled newspapers clutter the front porch. Signs that something is not right about this child's situation are illuminating. A strange car is parked in the driveway. Shades are pulled. He tries to remember the last time the mother or father was outside.

"Are you alone?" He whispers.

She shakes her head. "Daddy is with Mommy."

He looks into the girl's eyes, reflecting pools of sadness. A boulder rests in his stomach.

"Are they okay?" Liam asks. He wants to call for his mother, afraid of what this girl will say.

"My daddy told me to go outside for fresh air, " she says, twisting her hands. "Mommy is sick and is going home to be with the Lord."

A vortex of sorrow passes between the children as the girl's heartbreak becomes his. "But I don't want her to go to Him," she says, a sob embedded in her words. "I need her more than He does."

Liam embraces the little girl. His singular flame merges with hers. Every cell in his body holds the girl's emotions. The exquisite sense of loving kindness fills him in that moment of solidarity. So complete, it overflows, passing from him to the child he embraces to his father, now gone. Liam will soon understand the word empathy. There will be plenty of practice in comprehending the wounds in others, and he will remember his father's words. Love and kindness are potent healers.

# CHAPTER FOUR
# JOSEPH

As the van took a right turn on two wheels, its galvanized steel doors shuddered, threatening to come off their track. "Whoa, man. Slow down, okay?" The front-seat passenger shouts, though all the passengers can see he is laughing. "You flip this pony, and those guys will pray," he snickers, using his thumb to point to the rear. His grin is more of a sneer as he glances over his shoulder through a metal grill. The sullen inmates strapped in the back remain silent.

"They ain't getting out, brah," the driver says, and the two men laugh.

The vehicle doors aren't the only thing that shudders. Joseph Phung's stomach lurched so high that bile filled his mouth. He takes a deep inhale. *Please. Please. Not now.* Vomiting will cost him with his fellow passengers. He'd give anything for some blessed breeze. *Open the window.* His mind is screaming, but it's in vain. There are no windows. Only walls of steel, reinforced with meshed webbing.

Joseph is squeezed between two men who weigh at least fifty to sixty pounds more than him and have a height advantage of six or more inches. Though their hindquarters encroach on either side of his seat, he says nothing but continues to stare ahead, praying the contents of his stomach don't launch.

The driver and front passenger crack open their doors when the van pulls alongside a curb. A gush of fresh air is the most beautiful relief Joseph has ever experienced. *Thank you.* He breathes to any deity that might be listening. *Thank you*, he repeats as he places his hands folded in prayer, touching his thumbs to his forehead.

"Hey, Phung," the passenger yells. He is almost as broad as he is tall, with a heavy belly extending beyond the belt that holsters his gun. The sunlight catches the stubble that is resurfacing on his bald pate. The man is chewing tobacco or a wad of gum.

"Phung!" The guard bellows again with a bit more menace in his tone. "You can stop praying now. We made it." His laugh causes his girth to jiggle as he slides open the doors to the van. The daylight is overpowering, causing each passenger to shield their eyes. "Okay, ladies. Ya got a sunny day to do your civic duty. Jump out, grab a bag, and keep your distance from the friendly folks visiting the park."

Joseph takes in the tableau with his hand still covering his eyes. The park-goers' faces show that keeping space will not be a problem for him or his other companions as they collect debris from the property. People are moving away from the van and the inmates that emerge. *Who blames them?* Joseph thinks. With 'Chickasaw Federal Prison Camp' emblazoned across the van's panels, their arrival announces that a group of lepers has arrived.

The heat and humidity dials have been cranked as the prisoners walk single file around the park's parameters—their stiff, dark-blue uniform scratches against their moist skin as their bodies sweat. Joseph's black military-style boots pinch and weigh a couple of pounds as he marches. He's dragging a green plastic bag and a stick fastened with a hook. The other men are sporting sneakers purchased at the commissary—a luxury Joseph does not have, with no family or friends to support him.

As Joseph pierces wayward pieces of trash, he spies

a young girl sitting alone on a park bench. He swivels his head, looking in both directions and wonders if a parent is nearby. *If she were my child, I wouldn't leave her alone.* He freezes at the thought. *Who am I to make such a judgment?* He admonishes himself. His wife and son returned to Vietnam under a cloud of fear. He slides his rough hand across his face, hoping his tears pass for sweat. Once smooth as silk, those skilled hands understood the magic in the piano's heart. But those days are long gone and buried in the same plot as his hopes and dreams.

Joseph moves through the park, hooking debris and placing it in the bag. While the lack of breeze keeps the trash motionless, it doesn't help with the temperature. He stops again to wipe the perspiration dripping into his eyes and pulls the bill of his cap lower. As he does, he maintains an eye on the young girl, chatting adamantly with no one. *An imaginary friend*, Joseph thinks and smiles. *We can all use one.* Something is odd about the child's arm as she gesticulates. She is missing a hand.

The corners of Joseph's mouth turn down as he ponders what happened to this child and the unfairness of life - life's wheel of fortune. He married a wonderful woman and had an adoring boy. One minute, he was an up-and-coming pianist, performing at venues like the Lincoln Center and Carnegie Hall. He had just been hired to compose the soundtrack for a major studio. And then the wheel dipped.

\* \* \*

His agent invited Joseph for a contract signing celebration. The weather had turned foul, with rain dropping in sheets. Fog blanketed the city like an unrolling bale of cotton. Joseph called his wife to tell her about the meeting. "He wants to have one quick, celebratory drink. Thirty minutes, tops," he assured her.

"Be careful. It's pouring," his spouse warned.

The agent had a slighter build at five feet four inches and weighed under one hundred forty pounds. "Joseph," he hollered across the pub, waving his client to a standing-only table. A waiting platter of steaming snails made the pianist's stomach grumble, realizing he hadn't eaten the entire day. A bottle of Bia Saigon beer had been poured over ice and tantalized in the sweating mug. The ear-to-ear grin on the man's face was contagious as Joseph lifted the glass and said, "*Một, Hai, Ba, Vô*!!"

"Yes, cheers!" The agent raised his and clinked it against Joseph's.

"Have some." Joseph pointed to the plate but

recognized the man's squeamishness. "Okay." He grinned as he slurped the delicacy from their shells.

"You eat them like they're peanuts," he said as Joseph sucked and swallowed.

"Snails are popular in Vietnam," he said, picking up another.

"Not for me," the agent said, sipping his beer.

They spoke for about twenty-five minutes when Joseph checked his watch. "Hey, I've got to go. The wife will have me fried if I'm late again tonight." The two men shook hands, and the agent patted Joseph.

"You've made it, man. Congratulations. I am thrilled for you, Joseph." He offered his client a quick, awkward hug and waved goodbye.

* * *

Though Joseph wouldn't admit it aloud, the GMC Sierra 1500 was perhaps more truck than he could handle. Still, it was so *American* to be driving this masculine, tomato-red vehicle with a robust—*well, everything was robust about this truck*, he thought as the headlights fired on.

Although the wipers did their best to whoosh the

rain off the windshield, it was futile. Water poured onto the vehicle as if buckets had been loose from heaven. Tempted to turn on the radio, he thought better of it with the heavy fog and more traffic than expected. The clock on the dashboard announced he'd be late again.

Joseph was unaware of the slick asphalt surface as he drove along the street. He needed to get home and stepped on the gas. The tires could not contact the road with the increased speed. The truck hydroplaned as if possessing a mind of its own. His cell phone pounded the ominous Beethoven's 5th Symphony. He glanced down at its illuminated screen as it slid off his lap.

The impact moved in slow motion. The Sierra headed straight toward the car like a bullet from a gun. There was no missing the horrified face of the man whose head turned at the truck's oncoming lights. Joseph pressed on the brakes with all his might. Still, no amount of pressure was going to thwart the eventuality of the collision. He squeezed his eyes so tight they screwed into his head. He crossed his arms and whispered to any ancestor within hearing range. *Help.*

The police and firetruck arrived as if conjured from thin air. While Joseph tried to explain who he was and that this was a terrible accident, the policeman held the pianist's face flat against the asphalt pavement. A white sheet covered the man's body in his peripheral vision as the paramedics rolled it away. He pleaded, "Is he okay?" He was met with a sinister rebuke.

"How much did you have to drink tonight?" The policeman's accusatory stare pronounced Joseph guilty. His arms twisted behind his back, and he was handcuffed; the officer pushed him inside the police car.

If his life depended on it, Joseph could not recount what occurred between the time he left jail, stood before the court, was sentenced, and sent to Chickasaw Federal Prison Camp. No matter how many times he tried to replay the video of the moment, it was like watching the reel of someone else's life.

"Mr. Phung, I have accepted your plea of guilty," the judge said in a booming voice into the microphone. His black robe reminded Joseph of a raven swooping down to clean his bones. "On the night of January 5th, you were driving under the influence with a blood alcohol level of .03. Granted, not drunk. But impaired, you lost control of your vehicle and caused fatal harm."

Joseph blinked, trying to remember how much Bia Saigon beer he drank that night. One beer poured over ice, and he was sure he hadn't finished the mug. *I wasn't drunk! Does any of it matter? I'm here.* Joseph searched the courtroom as the judge droned on; no familiar face rallied or supported him.

"Mr. Phung." The judge's tone was annoyed by Joseph's lack of proper attention to the proceedings. "You took a congressman's life!" He shouted. "A congressman who leaves behind a wife and a young son. You have been charged with vehicular homicide, killing a public officer and a federal employee. This is a federal crime, and sentencing must be handled accordingly." The judge examined a pile of paper, shuffling it like a deck of tarot cards that held answers. "You will be remanded to the Federal Bureau of Prisons' custody, sentenced to six years, and a $50,000 fine." The judge banged his gavel, ending Joseph's day in court and encouraging the next case before the bench.

The bailiff lifted a numb Joseph from his seat, cuffed him again, and led him out of the courtroom. As they hustled him toward a waiting van, his court-appointed attorney placed a hand on his client's shoulder. "Wow, Joseph. Awesome news. You're going to 'ClubFed.' It's like a college campus. We couldn't have asked for a better outcome." The lawyer turned and left the shadow of his former client to confront his future alone.

\*\*\*

Six months into his sentence, Joseph Phung's life was upside down. If Chickasaw Federal Prison Camp was like a college campus, Joseph was sure of one thing: his attorney had never seen one. Rows and rows of bunk beds filled a cavernous room. Each inmate was issued the bare necessities: a few pairs of ill-fitting underwear, two blue uniforms, two T-shirts, and a pair of boots. Luxuries such as better toothbrushes, toothpaste, sweats, and tennis shoes were up to the inmate to purchase. Now a pariah to friends and family, these items would be far out of reach. With a $.10 per hour wage preparing fellow inmates to take their GED test, his wardrobe would not expand.

\*\*\*

"So, what you in for?" asked his new bunkmate. "Upper bunk." He instructed, pointing upward.

Joseph remembered his attorney's advice to stay mum about his crime but wasn't sure how to navigate the question. "Vehicular homicide," he mumbled as he climbed the few rungs to the top.

"Vehicular homicide?" the man's voice boomed. "Did you kill someone famous or his pet?" He laughed, expecting Joseph to join in. When none was forthcoming, he continued, "Sorry, man." He shook his head. "Better get yourself a sense of humor in here if you're gonna survive." He extended his weathered hand in Joseph's direction. "Name's Ridley, but everybody here calls me Bumpy."

The nickname needed no explanation, as Joseph noted the multiple bumps on the roommate's bald pate. Bumpy was a slight man. His sable skin shriveled like an old potato.

"Joseph." He returned the handshake. He was about to ask Bumpy why he was incarcerated and stopped. *Do I want to know?*

"How long is your bit?" Bumpy asked as he folded clothing and placed it in a locker.

"Sorry?" Joseph asked, unfamiliar with the slang.

"Your bit. How much time you got?" Bumpy asked again, amazed at his roommate's lack of understanding.

"Oh, six years." He pulled the wool blanket off his thin mattress and shuddered. Joseph did not want to say the words out loud. It made the total nightmare too real.

When Bumpy realized Joseph wouldn't ask about

his sentence, he volunteered, "Been here for ten. Ten more to go."

*Ten? Ten months?* Joseph thought, trying to calibrate the older man's meaning.

As if reading his roommate's mind, Bumpy said, "Done ten years. Got twenty but will be out in eight more. If I behave myself." For a man well into his sixties, he had the mischievous grin of a child and covered his mouth to hide his missing teeth.

Fear flashed through Joseph, wondering if the wheel of fortune had again dumped him into the same cell with an actual murderer. He held his tongue, not wanting to ask what crime had given this older man such a harsh sentence.

But as a man used to curious eyes and bored minds, Bumpy offered, "Drugs. Meth, to be exact. I didn't make it, but yeah, I sold some. A bad habit. Had it since about eleven." He scratched his head. "That meth is something bad. It…."

Before Bumpy finished, a guard stood in the doorway. "Follow your bunky, Phung. He'll show you the ropes. Just don't teach him any of your tricks, Bumpy." He winked and walked away.

Bumpy laughed. "He's a good one. Others, not so much. Power trip, if you ask me. They like authority a little too much. It gives them a sense of superiority, bossing everyone. Likely miserable at home with the missus. Some of them women guards are worse. Hoo-whew."

\* \* \*

A year into his sentence, Joseph understood that most incarcerated suffered from mental illness, homelessness, addiction, and bad choices. Yes, some inmates committed violent crimes, but like a river over rocks, that part of their nature had worn down. The number of young and old that passed through the prison camp like a revolving door amazed him. Some would find a way, but many others would return. For them, it became home.

Watching the feeble struggling to walk, Joseph wondered what purpose prison camp served. *How does society benefit from this? Who will these older men harm with their walkers, canes, nearly blind, and other maladies?* He also pondered how the younger ones would gain ground but accepted that incarceration had two roles—punishment and business.

"*Follow the money for the why of something,*" his grandfather had once advised.

\* \* \*

Though time creeps, Joseph learned to live in his six-by-eight-foot cinderblock cubicle. His teaching duties provided a sense of purpose and repaying his debt. *With education, the incarcerated have better odds of beating the cycle of incarceration.* He discovered that underneath Bumpy's quirky, rough demeanor was a thoughtful man.

"You've been here for what, Joseph? Three years?" Bumpy asked as they were cleaning their room.

"Like thirty," Joseph snorted. "But yes. Three years."

"Have you thought about the family of that congressman who died?"

Joseph froze. *Had I?* A rush of crimson colored his ears. In response, he studied his hands.

"Yeah, I know," Bumpy murmurs. "It's complicated. When something like this happens to you"—he waved around the room— "it's easy to think you're the only victim here. I mean, they got you, right? You lost everything—your friends. Hell, families turn their backs on you. It feels a lot better to feel sorry for yo-self. Somebody's gotta." His smile was wistful. "I spent my first ten years thinking about poor me, me, and me." Bumpy chuckled. "But after a while, that gets old. The would-of, could-of, and should-of run out of steam. You realize none of those matters. It happened, and you're here." He shuffled a deck of cards and dealt them.

"Sadness is like a tea bag, Joseph. Steep it too long in self-pity, and you end up with a heaping cup of victimhood." Bumpy studied the younger man's face. "I ain't going to lie, Joseph. I think you got a raw deal. Then again, everyone in this place, somewhere along the line, got a raw deal. Even worse than yours or mine. Horror stories. Some men have been abused beyond comprehension, been sexualized by a parent for drug money, or never had a home." He waved his hand. "I could go on and on. There will always be people with a lot worse going on than you could imagine."

The constant thrum of noise faded into the background as Joseph listened with rapt attention. Without realizing it, he had become self-absorbed in his wretched existence. *Did I think about my wife and son's lives and how they were doing, or indulge my misery of losing them, their abandonment?* How many nights had he wept for himself? The life he lost—the adoration, promise, and self-importance? *Plenty.* As this cantankerous older man spoke with such wisdom, Joseph cried. *It was an accident, but a man died.*

"I know," the older man soothed the roommate he called friend. "When you take a hard look at the wake of your actions…well, man, it's a killer." Bumpy patted Joseph on the back. "It forces you to acknowledge that you're not the only one suffering from fate's rerouting traffic cone. That accident altered other people's lives, too."

Joseph did not sleep that night. He tossed and turned, thinking about the vast web of people caught in the aftermath of it. His wife would have a different life in Vietnam, and his son would grow up without a father. So would the congressman's child. Joseph widowed a wife and orphaned a child. It was an accident, but accidents don't have soft landings.

In this dark room filled with snoring, feeble, and desperate men, Joseph realized his remorse and need for forgiveness had no opportunity to bloom. Every space within him brimmed with self-pity — until his heart opened, and light flowed in.

Joseph woke, excited about his epiphany. He had a fresh course, realizing what he owned and must do. The jangling of the guard's keys caused him to scurry down the ladder.

"Count!" The man's voice boomed.

Shocked that Bumpy was still asleep, Joseph shook his friend. "Bumpy, it's count." He shook him again. The roommate's mouth dropped open. His arm flopped to the side. "Bumpy?"

* * *

His last months in prison had arrived. Joseph thought about his wife and son. His heart ached, wondering if they were safe and flourishing. *Is my son growing well? Do they think of me?* He now understood how the weight of his guilt and shame twisted into a need for blame and victimhood.

"Sure, miss Bumpy," Joseph lamented to the inmate running the prison's library. "His heart gave out."

"Yeah, Bumpy might have been different, but he was one wise dude. He got it right in the end." The librarian replied as he paused. "Hmm," he said, scratching his head. "Do you think people can talk from the grave, Joseph?"

"I don't know. We revere our ancestors, but I don't know about talking…" He squinted a wary eye. "Why?"

"This book," the man said, pointing to the tome that had been returned. 'Forgiveness: Ask, Receive, Give.' From the worn book jacket, it was well-used. "Bumpy recommended it to everyone." He slid the book to Joseph. "Want it?"

"Sure," he said, grabbing it with two hands. "Think I have some time to read it." The two men chuckled.

As Joseph left the library, he noticed something—a treasure he had not seen in several years. An upright ebony piano was pushed against a wall. The door to the room where it stood was open. He turned to the librarian. "Did this piano just come?"

The man grinned. "Naw, man. It's been here before I came."

Joseph wondered how he missed it. *The eye will not see until the mind is ready.* "Would it be okay if I played?"

The librarian shrugged. "Don't anyone ever play that thing. It's so off-key that dogs will howl."

Joseph stepped into the room with reverence in the presence of the exquisite instrument. His fingers ached with longing. At least an inch of dust coated the keyboard and bench. He ran a finger over the keyboard cover—leaving his fingerprint in its wake. He inventoried the room, found a cloth, and began wiping down every nook and cranny of the once magnificent piece of craftsmanship.

"I'm so sorry they left you like this," he apologized to the piano.

When Joseph sat before the instrument, his hands rested upon the ivory. It was as if he never left. Time compressed the separation into this moment as his fingers remembered caressing the keys, running up and down scales. In gratitude for the attention, the piano was pitch-perfect. The keystrokes sent ethereal notes, causing prisoners and guards alike to stop, breathe, and listen.

Joseph wrote letters to everyone, asking for forgiveness. The hardest was the one for Congressman English's family.

"Phung," the guard yelled. "You've been assigned to clean up in the park. Vans outside."

* * *

Joseph pierces another piece of rubbish in the park. He checks the little girl as she stands up and brushes the collected pollen off her dress. He wonders if something is wrong with the child as she places her arms around thin air. But despite its oddness, she smiles and waves goodbye.

Dragging his trash bag and picking stick, Joseph catches the eyes of one guard and signals if it's okay for him to take a break. The guard points to his watch, raises his fingers, and gives a thumbs-up. Glad for the reprieve, he sweeps the remaining pollen off the bench and sits.

The branches of the tree offer a respite from the sun's heat. Reaching into his pocket, Joseph pulls a well-worn facecloth to wipe the accumulated sweat off his brow, neck, and face. The cloth is almost saturated.

Five years have passed since he entered Chickasaw. *Five years and five lifetimes ago.* There is an abyss of sorrow in prison. Men stare through walls watching their parents die, spouses and partners move on, children grow, and friends leave. The thought of entering a new world that has moved on is frightening. A world that doesn't recognize or want them.

He closes his eyes and remembers the man who died on that fateful night over five years ago. The horrified face still burned into the retina of Joseph's eyes, his soul, and his inability for self-forgiveness. He's thought about it over a million times. If he didn't go. Didn't have a beer. If he didn't watch the phone drop. But none of these thoughts would ever return the man from the grave. A tear slips from his eye and plops on his hand. Joseph studies the droplet. He wonders about the people affected by the accident and how many tears they shed. *It might create a lake.*

He sent the English family a letter asking for forgiveness. No reply. Then again, was Joseph expecting one? *Would I forgive anyone who killed my spouse or my father?* It saddens him in ways he cannot express. He would bear the scars of prison and the knowledge that he had taken a life.

The pianist bows his head to his chest and lets his mind wander up and down the keyboard. The music, like the wings of a bird, lifts him above the park, the van, the guards, and his fellow inmates. As his imagination grows more robust, someone pats his shoulder. He opens his eyes. The blaze of the sunlight hits him. Joseph tilts his head back, thinking the guard is calling him back. "Oh," he says. "I thought I had a couple more minutes." He replaces his baseball cap, blocking the rays of the sun. He startles and leans away from the man. *It couldn't be!* He tries to convince himself. Joseph considers the face again, blinks harder, and stares again. "Congressman English?" Like a mirage on a hot summer day, the man's figure shimmers, ethereal with brilliance.

"Are you coming to take your revenge?" Joseph asks, chewing his lower lip, wondering if this specter will drag him into the bowels of an underworld. *Has Địa Mẫu, the Mother Earth Goddess of the Dead, come to reclaim me?* His body quakes with fear, yet he stretches his arms before him. "I surrender."

As Joseph exhales a sigh, he crumbles. "I've been waiting for you," he says, looking into Phillip English's face. "Surprised you waited this long. I wouldn't have—if you killed my wife." He bows his head and shakes it side to side. "Revenge is sweeter knowing I leave prison in two weeks. I deserve it. So, let's go." Joseph stands up and extends his hand to this stranger.

The stranger stretches out his hand and touches Joseph's arm. "I am not here for revenge, Joseph. I am here for forgiveness." The nimbus of light surrounding Phillip English sways as he moves his head.

He takes Joseph in his arms and flies through the darkest clouds the pianist had ever imagined. A sense of foreboding pulsates through the atmosphere. Rising into the heavens is the din of wailing. "Someone is crying," Joseph says, becoming alarmed.

"Everyone who has died is crying." The stranger returns.

Joseph shudders, wondering if he is destined for a painful death. "Why are they crying if they're dead?"

"They are experiencing the totality of their life. The

joy they brought, the love they shared, and the pain and suffering they caused."

When Joseph peers down, endless firepits cover the ground. Some are smoldering, and others have flames leaping thirty feet or more. He clings tighter now to Phillip English, afraid this might be his destination. *Killing me brings forgiveness?* He trembles. "Are you bringing me here to suffer?" Joseph asks with a quaking voice. "Is forgiveness forged by fire? I'd rather fall from this height than burn," he pleads.

The silence between them is an eternity. "Can you see what is happening in those burning pits, Joseph?"

Joseph buries his head against the stranger's chest, too fearful of confronting the scene. "No," he whimpers.

The stranger braces the pianist's body closer to his chest and dips into sight of the pits. "And now, Joseph?"

Secure in this man's arms, Joseph opens his eyes and gasps. Humans remove their bodies, shedding them like old clothing and placing them into the flames. Freed orbs emerge, converging with other orbs of light. What was once their bodies were cremated into ashes, leaving no trace. "People are discarding their bodies!" Joseph's voice filled with more awe than fear.

He is in stunned disbelief as these lights climb and dance, colliding and separating, floating past and through him. Joseph takes a sharp breath as an orb enters him. He is replete with a love that spills from his body, yearning to join the orbs.

"Before your spirit returns to Oneness, you leave behind the human form and its pride. Within pride lives all the evils committed during a lifetime. This is where the individual consciousness dies and turns to ash. For some humans, this is the hell they believe in, where evil, like Hitler, Stalin, Bundy, Zedong, and others go. But as you can see"—he points to the fire pits— "all humans enter the flames because all have committed some wrong. And the dead will bury their dead. The soul is once again liberated to its original form - love."

Joseph is speechless.

"Love cannot hold grudges, does not seek recompense for wrongs, nor desires revenge. Giving and receiving forgiveness are essential to healing. With self-loathing and an unwillingness to forgive yourself, you will never move beyond that moment. Never heal. You cannot give forgiveness or accept the forgiveness of others if you do not give it to yourself. It is like giving and receiving an apple but never having tasted one. You cannot recognize what you are giving or receiving. And even if someone withholds their forgiveness, you must still forgive yourself."

"I don't deserve forgiveness." Joseph's head went limp against the stranger's chest.

They flew away from the fire pits and arrived at the intersection of that dark and rainy night. Joseph clung to the stranger. "Please," he begs. "Please don't bring me here. I can't."

But the stranger held Joseph closer to the scene to witness the accident from a distinct vantage point. "Open your eyes, Joseph, but see with your heart."

\* \* \*

The rain was torrential. Every square inch of Joseph's body ached from the impact. He pushed against the deployed airbag and unlatched the door. *I've got to help that man!* Even if he must crawl through the soupy fog. When he opened the truck door, the cell phone fell out. Joseph lifted it and turned on the flashlight. "Hello," he called out, though his head was swimming. Silence. "Hello," he cried out.

A faint voice croaked. "Help."

Joseph rushed in the sound's direction. His hand touched the crushed car. He shined the light on the face, smeared with blood. He gasped, covering his mouth to stifle nausea and shock. "Let me help you." The steering wheel crushed the man. Joseph moved to open the door, but the man's hand touched his arm.

"Don't. Please. Don't move me." His eyes clouded, but Joseph caught a tiny flame within them.

"I can help you, please."

Phillip was begging now. "No. As I approached the intersection, my heart… but I didn't have the strength to stop the car. I'm sorry." His voice was raspy and fading. "Tell Liam I love him." He coughed and turned away. Joseph checked for Phillip English's pulse—none.

\* \* \*

"I didn't kill him?" Joseph asks the stranger who brought him back to the day that changed his life. "It was an accident. I didn't mean to…"

"The blame does not matter. It is finished and cannot be undone. What matters is now. You have compassion and sorrow for the life lost and the effects on his family and yours. Everyone misses the mark, Joseph. It's what you do afterward that matters. Offer the same grace to yourself. That same love and forgiveness you are learning to ask for and provide to others."

They return to the park bench. The glow expands from the man's body and blends in with the ambient light.

"What must I do?" he asks before the stranger vanishes.

"Show Liam his father's love."

"Are you Phillip English?"

"I am—who you need me to be."

\* \* \*

The door to the building swings open. As Joseph walks past the final checkpoint, a guard gives him the few personal possessions held and twenty-five dollars in cash. "Hope we don't see you again, Phung," a woman yells, snapping her gum and never making eye contact.

He was going to say, "Don't worry. You won't." But he offered no words. What would be the point? After all, prisons need returning inmates to stay in business; many would accommodate this need.

Joseph is wearing khaki pants and a short-sleeved polo shirt. A relief from the starched-laden blue uniform. He inhales as the sun's warmth beams across his face. A car is waiting beside the sidewalk, and he quickens his pace. His spouse and son are here. The boy has grown almost as tall as his father. They rush to meet and embrace him in a hug. When they join, there is one heartbeat.

\* \* \*

His wife dusts the new piano in the family room. It is secondhand and well-used. "It's beautiful. Thank you," Joseph says as he squeezes her closer.

"Thank you for everything." She bows. "For your forgiveness, Joseph. We didn't mean to leave you, but we were so afraid."

He kisses her lips. "I love you."

The wife smiles and opens a newspaper. Above the fold, Joseph reads an announcement about his return to music and offering piano lessons. "You'll have more students than you want." She puts the paper down. "Tea?"

He nods. As she goes into the kitchen, the doorbell rings. When he looks through the glass, he spots the profile of a younger person of about twelve or thirteen waiting on the front porch. His shaggy corn silk blond hair glints with sunlight.

Joseph opened the door wide, catching the older boy off guard.

"Oh. Hi," the boy mumbles, looking down at his feet. "You're the new piano teacher giving lessons?"

"Yes. Come in." The boy's face reminds him of someone. *Perhaps a fellow musician's child?* "I'm Joseph Phung," he says, offering his hand.

"Yes, I know, " he replies, returning the shake. I'm Liam English, Phillip's son." His father's words come through. *Anger that has a beginning must have an end.*

Joseph pauses. "I'm so sorry, Liam. Your father loves you."

Liam looks into the teacher's eyes and says, "I know." He pulls a sheet of music from his knapsack. "This might be weird, but can you teach me to play 'My Heart Will Go On?' My mom is always humming and singing. I want to play it for her."

Joseph takes the sheet and glances at the lyrics. "You are safe in my heart, and my heart will go on…." He places his hands on Liam's shoulders. "Love lives on and on."

# Chapter Five
# Cotton

The pain radiating from his hip to his foot reminds him he has aged. He swears that groans now accompany the typical crackling of his bones as if his weight is a burden. "What are you complaining about?" he scolds his body like an incorrigible child. "I don't weigh but a minute."

He isn't exaggerating. His ribs are revealed from front to back at one hundred twenty pounds and just under six feet. An arthritic hand runs down his legs. Gingerly, he places one leg over the side of the bed and plants his foot. "That's right." He commands his limbs as he swings his second leg to catch up.

The older man shuffles along the well-worn wooden floor, planting one foot before the other as if dancing.

He eyes his aluminum walker with bright yellow tennis balls attached to its legs and shakes his head. "Later." He informs the device. A hand trembles, but he's more irritated than concerned when his coffee sloshes back and forth in his cup. "Let's not waste it." He advises his quaking fingers.

\* \* \*

Booker Taliaferro Mathers was born in 1921 in Macon, Georgia. Though named after Booker T. Washington, one of America's most influential African Americans, his nickname, Cotton, stuck. As he would learn, Cotton arrived on the same day as the Tulsa Race Massacre, when almost three hundred Black Tulsans were gunned down. An angry mob of White neighbors torched the affluent neighborhood of Greenwood, leaving a thirty-five square block area in smoking ruin. While Cotton's family lived about a thousand miles away from this event, they understood racial terrorism, discrimination, and outright denial of trying to make a life.

The year before Cotton arrived, his father, Hiram Mathers, planned to move north, joining the Great Migration. Rumors circulated about factories and opportunities opening in Minnesota. "Minnesota?" Minnie

Mathers questioned her husband. "Doesn't it freeze?" She asked, wrapping her arms across her chest and feigning a shiver.

"I'd rather be cold and have hope, Minnie, than warm and go nowhere." They began packing and planning for their route north. News of a hanging in Duluth, accompanied by a photo of White faces smiling at the bodies hanging from trees, caused the couple to rethink their plan. "They're lynching here in Georgia," Hiram said as they unpacked their belongings. "But going to Minnesota might be going from the frying pan into the fire."

The husband smoothed his finger across Minnie's furrowed brow as she covered her swollen belly. "If our child is a son, he will not be a sharecropper," Hiram shook his head. Sharecropping is a fancier word for slavery."

Minnie touched her husband's arm. "We need to go north."

"We will when the time is right."

Two weeks later, when a fourteen-year-old Black child was accused of stealing, the time had come. Though the boy denied the allegations, they erected makeshift gallows and mouths salivated at the thought of a hanging.

When a White man whom Hiram befriended came to the child's defense, the mob lynched him as well. Bodies swayed from tree limbs with a layer of rope coiled around their throats. Hiram thought *blood-thirsty people would sacrifice any soul at the altar of their wickedness.* Panicked, he rushed home and couldn't catch his breath. "We need to leave tonight, Minnie." His chest heaved so hard that his wife thought her husband's heart might stop.

"Tonight?" Beads of perspiration swelled across her face. "The baby is due any day."

Stung by the reality of her words, Hiram's panic slowed. "Right after this baby is born, we're leaving. If White people are killing each other for standing up to evil, we cannot raise a child here. And folks call the boll weevil vile." He shook his head.

Hiram, Minnie, and their infant son, Cotton, boarded a bus bound for Philadelphia. As the vehicle rolled north, the landscape whizzed by. With distance behind them, they breathed a long sigh. Hiram gripped Minnie's hand. "Philadelphia was the headquarters of America's fight for freedom from the British. It'll be the right place for our child."

\* \* \*

The tremor in Cotton's hand calms as he clasps the coffee mug. His Russell Terrier, Winston, is lying at his owner's feet, head looking up with a sweet, practiced beggar's face. Cotton's little dog hopes a few morsels will be dropped in his direction. Cotton bends, and every millimeter of the stretch aches. He drops a piece of biscuit near the dog's face. "You can still smell, but I'll make it easier for you, boy," he says, rubbing between the animal's ears. "Wish somebody would do the same for me." Cotton chuckles.

He's been sitting in the chair too long. Pins and needles crawl up his legs. Winston whines, reminding Cotton he's ready for a walk. "Okay. Give me a second. At this age, you need patience." With his feet planted, Cotton rocks side to side, hoping momentum will aid the lift. He catches the walker's accusatory stare. "You're right," he concedes. "Should have used you." He nods, acknowledging his gaffe to the device.

Much as he hates admitting it, Cotton realizes he needs more help. The doorbell now whispers. The stairs are steeper, and even making toast is a chore. His dog shakes its arthritic hips. "You are almost fifteen years old, Winston. In human years, you're one hundred and three, the same age as me. We are both moving slower." With his hands flat on the table, Cotton pushes off, stands, and wobbles. He wishes the walker would come to him.

\* \* \*

No one is more shocked than Cotton that he has lived this long. "I didn't have a monastic life," he confided to a friend one day while they played chess in the park. I liked an excellent whiskey, a smoke or two, and staying out late. Guess I must have gotten the right bingo card." He laughed, but underneath the smile was the deep ache of a man whose entire family- wife, child, and only grandchild- died before him.

"Lucky?" he asks, his aged face in the mirror. "Or cursed." Through his rheumy eyes, Cotton does not recognize the man staring back. His once handsome face now resembles a collapsed prune. The bronze shine to his brown skin is now grayish. A dark-haired Afro that swayed in his youth is gone.

The woman who cleans his home left a photo album within Cotton's reach. It had been a while since he flipped through the picture book his mother Minnie assembled. His mother and father doted on him as an only child. They recorded all his milestones with Minnie's Kodak Brownie camera.

As Cotton turns the yellowed pages, he understands his parents' sacrifices for a better life. A picture floats to the floor. He weighs his curiosity against the pain that will follow when he bends to pick it up. Curiosity wins. The photograph takes his breath away. Though he had seen it many times, nothing would ever defuse the bestial capacity of humans. Cotton stares at the image of three Black men stripped to the waist with a rope tied around their necks. The Duluth, Minnesota lynching. His mother and father kept it as a reminder of vigilance.

Cotton glares at the jeering and gleeful faces of the people and wonders how humanity embraces such psychopathy. *Just because a mob or a nation agrees to kill doesn't make it right.* He saw the picture before when his parents reminded him that, despite living up north, it didn't end animus and brutality. Cotton exhales and places the photo back in the album. Neither geography nor time eliminates that hatred. He witnessed the same tableau of men in crisp uniforms cheering as emaciated Jews swung from ropes.

\* \* \*

In 1944, Cotton enlisted in the army, joining the fight in World War II. He reported for duty after a long, tearful goodbye to his parents. He was assigned to the US 12th Armored Division—one of only ten US divisions that integrated combat companies during World War II. Though segregated at home, Black and White soldiers bonded on the battlefield. The unit arrived in Liverpool, England, and then fought in France, Germany, and Austria in the European Theater of Operations. As they died in combat, Cotton and the men fighting beside him understood that all the blood flowing across the earth was red despite their skin color, ethnicity, or ideology.

It struck Cotton that few men found killing a natural thing. He would later read 'Marshall's Men Against Fire' and discover that only one in four fired their weapons while in contact with the enemy. He wondered why peace was so elusive. Why did nations go to war, and humans went along with it? *Sure, demons like Hitler had to be stopped,* he thought, after he returned home from the military. *But why do we insist on wars?* As he sat in his living room, the horrors of the Vietnam War unfolded on his color television.

Cold sweat dripped down his back. Cotton wanted to avoid inviting these images into his house. Images prompted too many flashbacks. As he stood to shut off the TV, his wife, Lillian, walked into the room and handed him cool water. The woman had an uncanny ability that amazed Cotton.

"Lots of boys won't be coming back." Her sullen

tone filled the room with an air of foreboding. "It won't be a comfort to their mothers that they died in service to their country. No folded American flag is going to bring their child back."

Cotton downed the drink and studied her as she retrieved the glass from him.

"I'm not being disrespectful, Cotton. I have the utmost respect for our soldiers and recognize their sacrifices going into the military. When you came home from the war…." She examined her hands. Something inside you, Cotton, changed. Whatever you experienced, I guess you never want to experience it again. It took away a piece of you," she said.

Lillian was right. Cotton left the romanticism of war on the battlefield and replaced it with an intimate understanding of its realities and the human capacity for evil. "War," he mumbled.

"I don't understand, Cotton. Killing each other, blowing up the earth and its people. Why Cotton? Why?" She shook her head and dabbed her eyes with a handkerchief.

"We go to battle believing we are on the right side. Avenging angels. Like needing to take down Hitler and now communism." He paused and rubbed the graying hair. "But you're right, Lillian. In a few years, something else will start one, then something else. We want to believe we'll stomp out the vile people doing bad things, but I'm not so sure anymore."

The corners of his mouth turned down. "Are we turning into those people that must be stopped?" He placed his arms around her shoulder and walked her into the kitchen. "I earned my college degree with the GI Bill and enjoy accounting almost as much as I do your cooking." His crooked smile caused her to return a grin. "Numbers are straightforward. They say, 'yes or no,' 'black or white.' War is anything but." He took the glass from her hand and put it in the sink.

"I understand what you're saying, Cotton. I once believed *we* were the heroes. Now…." Her voice trailed off. She took his hand. "Humans have been battling with each other since the dawn of time. And I'm afraid war won't end…until we do." Lillian took her husband's hand. "Cotton, you're nearing fifty, so they won't call you again." She breathed a hollow chuckle. "You better than most remember. You can help those soldiers."

At this point in his life, Cotton didn't think about helping, let alone returning military personnel. The demons from twenty-five years ago still lingered in the recesses. A car backfiring. The flash of a camera bulb. Little things triggered the rush of anxiety, bringing the battlefield fresh into his mind. Still, he thought, *if anyone understood the journey home.*

Cotton remembered arriving stateside. The jubilation of V-J Day marked the end of World War II. The ticker tape parades where African Americans joined comrades of different races to march with pride. But if Cotton was honest with himself, the victory was not about defeating the enemy. Coming back to his friends and family outside a coffin was something to celebrate. The relief that he came home in one piece.

"You're right, Lillian. I need to step up. They welcomed us as heroes when we returned from World War II. People couldn't give us enough praise. The soldiers returning from Vietnam… it's rough. Won't be any parades for them."

Cotton dedicated several days a month. Each soldier suffered some wounding. The older man's angst over war and the carnage in its wake grew with years of volunteering.

\* \* \*

Fifteen years later, Cotton and Lillian retired from their jobs and planned a long cruise. Before they packed, an aneurysm claimed Lillian's life at sixty-five.

"Lil," he said to his wife's photo one evening. Sometimes, I don't think I can do this anymore." He continued his chatter as he removed his shoes, tie, watch, and belt. But then, somebody's got to do it. So why not me? Somebody's got to love those soldiers and assure them they didn't lose an arm, a leg, or a friend for no reason."

He leans into her photograph. "Lil, I'm not sure I can offer a reason. The military and arms industry are partners. Business needs war." He kisses the picture, climbs into his empty bed, and turns off the light on the nightstand. "Night, sweetheart."

\* \* \*

Cotton lives in the same house he and Lillian purchased seventy-five years ago. *You'd 'a been one hundred and four today*. He smiles, thinking about the only woman he's ever loved. "Some folks would have said you robbed the cradle." He laughs, but it dissolves into a cough. Winston is now creeping back and forth over Cotton's feet, reminding him about that walk. "Hold your horses," he says to the pet. He grabs the leash, snaps it onto the collar, and opens the screen door. "Now, don't be pulling me down those steps, Winston. Otherwise, this might be our last one."

The warmth of the sun spreads across his back and down his arms. Although gnarled, Cotton can still stretch his fingers. He drops Winston's lead, knowing the faithful friend won't leave his side. Not because of the animal's arthritic joints but because from the first day Cotton brought him home from the shelter, this animal understood the man's grief and loneliness.

"Morning, Mr. Cotton," a neighbor boy hollers as the elderly man and his ancient dog pass.

"Morning to you," Cotton calls back, though his voice is not as robust. The child with trim-cut hair, espresso skin, and gentle brown eyes mounts his bicycle, waves, and rides off.

Cotton wonders what type of world this young man will encounter. The older man believes he witnessed it all on this planet in one hundred and three years. From lynchings and outright hatred because of skin color to the election of the first Black president. He smiles at the thought of the inauguration and only wishes Lillian lived to cherish the day. Still, one election doesn't change the hearts and minds of a nation about race, differing ideologies, or religious beliefs.

With people willing to follow, presidents can incite a division not seen since the Civil War. As he shuffles, he thinks. *Are we heading for one?* He wonders about that boy again and how he's sure the child's parents had 'the talk' with their son about being a Black man in America. He shakes his head at this idea and grabs Winston's leash as they prepare to cross the street. Crossing requires more time than the traffic light's countdown will give.

When the duo arrives, the park is quiet for a sunny morning. A few children walk with their caregivers, holding hands and pointing. Melancholy fills Cotton as he moves along, saddened by what the generation of today will face.

While so much has changed in America since 1921, some of the most important things have not altered to the degree needed. Human behavior was at the top of the list. He wipes at a surprise tear that rolls down his face. *Mass shootings that murder children and innocent bystanders. And hatred. Why do we insist on self-destruction?* The thought exhausts him. As if sensing Cotton's weariness, Winston pulls the wizened man toward a bench.

"Thank you, Winston. You're a loyal friend and a

smart dog." He wishes he placed some biscuits in his jacket pocket. "I love you even if I don't give you treats, right?" The dog pants and smiles at the man he loves.

Cotton is tiring and winded. He slides back against the bench and inhales, trying to steady the flow of his breath. The tremor in his hand kicks in, and he cups the other hand over it for calm. He closes his eyes and thinks about what his hundred–year life has witnessed. *Can you believe a man would walk on the moon?* He yawns, leans back, and tucks his arms behind his head. "A man without a care in the world," Lillian would tease.

"Winston," he says to the dog stretched out beside him to enjoy the sun's warmth. "Who'd ever thought we would talk into watches like Dick Tracy? And that internet." He lets out a slow, almost whistle. "It answers anything and everything." He strokes Winston's wiry fur. "Me, I'm too old to be worried about it. Old dogs can't learn new tricks. Right, Winston?" He snorts as the animal pops his head up.

As the sun warms Cotton's face, the muscles throughout his body relax. He is stretched out further than he has been in a long time. His breath is steady with the rhythmic beating of his heart. "Winston. Despite not understanding so many things about life and all its valleys, life has been sweet," he whispers. He closes his eyes, hoping to rest for a few minutes.

A younger African American man with reddish brown skin sits beside Cotton. His chocolate eyes sparkle. "Wow," he exclaims. "You sure got old." He covers his mouth to stifle a chuckle.

Roused from his sleepiness, Cotton opens his eyes. The sun is too bright for the hour. The older man raises his hand, covering his eyes. "Are you talking to me?" he asks, still blinded by the brilliance.

"Yes, sir." The tone is chipper, without a hint of sarcasm. "How old are you?" the man continues to probe.

Displeasure crosses Cotton's face. *Then again, I was once a talkative, curious man. H*e thinks before he responds. "You might not believe me, but I'm a hundred and three." Satisfaction fills his voice with a slight lifting of his chin.

"That's a lot of mileage," the specter exclaims with genuine admiration.

"Yup." Cotton agrees. The light falls behind the man's form, and Cotton focuses on the young visitor. "Name is Cotton," he says, stretching out his hand. He pats his sleeping dog. "This here is Winston. Guess he's beat." He offers an excuse for the dog's lack of manners.

The younger man stretches out his hand and clasps Cotton's. He doesn't offer his name, but as the two connect, a flow of energy courses through the older man's body. Every cell is rejuvenated and alive.

Cotton rubs his eyes. Though his vision has deteriorated over the past few decades, he focuses on the youthful face. Something is so familiar about this stranger that Cotton's stomach flutters. He inches back a bit and takes in the face again. "I'd swear you were my son, but I only had one child—a daughter." Believing his eyes are deceiving him, he rubs one more time. When he moves his hands away, the face comes into focus.

"You look like me, except eighty years younger." He leans in to study the visitor's face, trying to confirm his suspicion but hoping this is just a dream. "So, uh… what brings you here?" Cotton asks to determine whether the man is real or his imagination.

"You asked me to be here," the young man replies matter-of-factly.

"I don't remember inviting you," Cotton says with indignation.

"You still have a lot of unanswered questions at, um. …" He pauses.

"A hundred and three." He interrupts. Though unaware, Cotton's hands grip Winston tighter, hoping the dog will infuse courage into his frail old man's body. "Yes, I have lots of questions about life. But isn't this in reverse? If I can't answer them by a hundred and three, how do you, at twenty-something, think *you* can?" Cotton replies, rallying his smugness as if age gives him the edge. "Besides, isn't the older, wiser self supposed to advise the younger self?"

"Naw, that's a myth. If your older self talked to your younger self, you wouldn't be yourself. You'd have taken all kinds of different paths."

"Hmm," Cotton ponders. "I guess you're right about that."

"Well, why don't you try some questions?" the visitor suggests.

Cotton takes a deep breath. He thinks about the boy from his neighborhood. "Okay. Here's one. You're a young Black man. Why is race such a source of hatred?" A smile creeps across Cotton's face, and he believes he stymied his new companion.

"No softballs?" the man winks and shrugs his shoulders. "Before I begin, let me ask you one question first."

Cotton squints one eye. "Humph. Where's this conversation going?" He flushes at his annoyance. "Sorry. Ask away," he concedes.

"Where do you think humans come from?" The man's face is sincere, without mockery or arrogance.

The genuineness of this stranger surprises him. Cotton responds. "God."

The young man says nothing but nods.

"Well, is that right?" Cotton asks, exasperation creeping back.

"God, Allah, Jehovah, Yahweh, Source, Brahma, Universe, Creator, or any of the many names given to that which creates. Humanity is created by transforming a particle from the One into a sentient being–a spark of Light. Beings that can experience life in ways the intangible cannot. All particles are from the same Universal Source." He closes his eyes and places his palms on his thighs.

Cotton waits and scratches his bald pate. Knowing this is the man's answer, he asks, "So if I'm getting this straight, humans are each a piece of the Universe?" His pitch rises.

The visitor nods his head and holds up one finger. "Yes, with one exception. You use the word, *each* as if humans are separate. They are not. But to have a tangible encounter, particles incarnate to interact with the world and experience life in physical ways—the cry of a baby, the vows of union, the mourning of death. Humans are created from love and born to bring it into existence.

"Wait a minute,"—Cotton cocks one eyebrow— "If you're telling me that humans are love… then why are we such a malicious species? Our actions are far from *that*." His stomach churns, building anger. "Just study history. We've been killing each other since Cain and Abel."

His entire body quivers with loss and sadness. *Why would a loving God want this?* Cotton sighs and searches the specter's warm brown eyes. "If a Higher Power knows we will do heinous things, why doesn't he stop us? Why would he allow wickedness?"

"The Divine doesn't create evil, Cotton. Human agency, its free will, does. If the Creator stepped in and selected which actions were acceptable, would humanity have free will? Choice can manifest acts of wickedness, but it also offers courage, mercy, and kindness. You cannot eliminate one without the other. Do you understand?" The young visitor searches Cotton's face.

"I suppose," Cotton replies with a sigh.

"Humans fall asleep to their connection to the Divine and each other."

Cotton pauses. "So how…where did we go wrong?"

"It begins with the illusion of separateness. Difference. The ego grows, often creating a perception of superiority. Seeing difference as inferior gives license to hate, reduce, and even kill."

Cotton's curiosity is piqued. "But we are separate." He raises his hand. "I'm separate from you." He pauses and catches the younger man's smile.

"The Creator imbues sentient beings with egos to create a *sense* of self. This allows you to experience things. But the ego is encased in a shell of humility, preventing it from growing. The connection to the Divine stays intact." He stops.

Cotton nods in encouragement, steepling his fingers.

"Humans call ego free will. People make choices—good, bad, and both." He casts his eyes down at Winston and smiles. Humans are not born with hate or predisposed to prejudice. Younger children look beyond differences into the soul. They recognize each other there. Then, their tiny, budding egos are taught to believe that being different makes them better, and superiority begins!

Cotton nods. "Yes, it does."

"It's an addiction that must be fed. Soon, the ego grows beyond its shell of humility and becomes pride. Once it breaks through, boundaries are removed. "He strokes Winston. "Dogs have egos. But unlike humans, they remain humble and are loving and forgiving. Of course, human cruelty interferes with this balance."

Winston sighs, and both men laugh. "I think old Winston outgrows his shell from time to time." Cotton's bittersweet smile conveys the knowledge that man and dog are running out of time. "Nah. I'm just messing with you. Winston is a loyal companion. Real good friend." He shifts the precious bundle closer.

"Humans say, 'You must have pride!'" But it's wrong. Pride is the liar, the tempter, and deadly. It worms its way into humans and cloaks the connection to God. Hubris creates the illusion of separateness from others. Once set loose…" He sighs and hangs his head down.

"Finish your thoughts," Cotton pushes.

"It causes humanity's sins—lust, greed, sloth, anger, envy, and gluttony. Greed feeds war, while gluttony wastes and starves people in need. Anger holds weapons to murder the masses, lust fuels rape, envy steals, and sloth allows humans to slumber through all of this," he laments. "Pride spins the lie that one person, religion, and institution is the authority on truth. Anyone who opposes this is wrong. There is no greater evil than to hate reasonable discourse. Friends, families, and communities no longer have discussions, a willingness to listen, and tolerance for other ideas. Many paths lead to God, but only to one destination. Death is an excellent equalizer."

The older man shakes his head. "You're speaking facts. So, why keep creating humans?" As Cotton studies the younger face, a light emerges.

The younger man's body grows brighter. "Humanity isn't a failed project, Cotton. Despite the world's evils, humanity still offers love. Not because they fear punishment but because they remember who and what they are. There is no greater power when love struggles against wrongs and breaks through. It repairs the world.

"Age makes you cynical." Cotton's disappointment is palpable.

A brilliant beam, as if staring into the sun, surrounds

them. Reflexively, Cotton squints, eyes watering from the stinging brilliance. Tendrils of fear grip him. His hand reaches to find Winston, the young man, or any passerby to grab hold. A loud 'whoosh' rushes past him as if he is in the center of a tornado, and then a huge 'pop.'

Absolute silence, calm, and peace envelop him. Cotton opens his eyes to velvet blackness. Decillion lights are twinkling around him, floating over him, through him, embracing him. He stretches one hand free and touches an orb of light. His mother, Minnie. She is so close that her beating heart thumps against his. Another orb floats. His father, Hiram, smiles, rubs his son's dark, curly hair, and embraces him in the bear hug Cotton has missed for years.

The cacophony of exploding grenades and gunfire sounds. He is kneeling on the battlefield, holding the hand of a dying comrade and whispering prayers of comfort. Cotton makes his way through a forest, rifle at the ready. He stumbles upon a young German soldier who is relieving himself. Cotton raises his gun, aiming at the frightened man who is his exact age. The man says, "Bitte. Please," as he lifts his hands. Cotton lowers the gun. Mercy flows through his veins. Surrounded by darkness, the pages of Cotton's life are turning.

"More?" A voice asks.

He nods and whispers, "Please." Lillian appears. She is wearing that beautiful ivory dress. She reaches for his hand, and Cotton is not saying those vows but sensing them with every fiber of his being—the wail of a newborn baby. "A girl," someone shouts, bringing Cotton to his knees. His heart is bursting from so much love that a bridge of light extends from him to his daughter as he witnesses her grow, give birth, and both mother and child die. Yet the bridge of illumination continues. Lillian is smiling and kissing his lips when she collapses. Cotton's heart breaks again at this immeasurable loss, but the halo of their bond remains.

The pages of Cotton's life continue to flip.

A soldier on crutches hobbles in. The man lost a leg to war. He rests his head on his newfound friend's shoulder and sobs. Cotton assures him, "You'll be fine. You'll see." The man runs with an athletic prosthesis to pick up his child. *No, not his child,* Cotton corrects himself. He understands now that the soldier became a pediatric oncologist, saving many lives.

Reliving the moment, Cotton stands at attention.

Soldiers form a line, waiting for Cotton's infamous hug. Some are returning home to divorce, have trouble finding work, suffer unending nightmares of war, or have ill partners to care for. Each person sobs into the older man's chest as he listens and provides a state of grace for them.

Cotton is floating above the room. A female officer with a loaded gun places it near her temple. She is the lone survivor of a bomb attack. The weight of her shame jars through him. He rests his hand on hers. "Turn this guilt into something useful. Somebody just like you needs to hear your message." She puts her weapon away, and he recognizes she has become a speaker for suicide prevention.

The sandpapery lick of his dog. A desperate puppy in a shelter. A clock is ticking for adoption or euthanasia. The beautiful face of Winston, the companion who saved him from despair with kisses that licked a hundred wounds and a thousand tears, helped Cotton move forward.

He rubs his eyes and the pit of his stomach calms. *I never knew my life had this much meaning.*

The young stranger says, "When life passes before you, you understand how those moments create a ripple effect. So, humans are created, Cotton—to love. When the journey ends, it is the only thing returning to the Source. Pride and all its evils die on the threshold of the Universe.

"Are you me?" Cotton asks.

"I am—who you need me to be." The younger man smiles and rests a hand on Cotton's shoulder.

* * *

Twins are running around the park. They spy the man and his pet sitting still on the bench. Their curiosity grows as they inch forward—a gentle breeze riffles through the dog's fur. The man's spotted and wrinkled hands envelop the animal. They step closer. "Can we pet your dog, mister?" They ask. There is only silence.

# Chapter Six
# Kip

Kip Homestead glides the razor across his stubbled jawline. These days, fewer tissues are needed to stem the nicks. Eyes closed, he grabs a face towel and blots away remnants of shaving cream. When he opens them, Lara's reflection is in the mirror.

"Hi, handsome," she says with a playful smile. Her face is beautiful. Free from illness and suffering.

*Lara.* Energy radiates from her as though her presence is physical. *I miss you, babe.* She waves and vanishes.

Kip lifts his chin, checking for any errant whiskers. Luster has returned to his hair and catches the light.

Trimmed and styled, ten years have been erased from his face. He flaps a striped, blue button-down shirt, making a 'snapping sound,' slips it on, and fastens the last button. Grabbing a tie, the man's fingers twist like pipe cleaners to make a knot. *Still a bit rusty. Lara was great with ties.* The widower retrieves his coat, gives the apartment one final sweep, turns off the lights, and locks the door behind him.

* * *

Over five years have passed since his wife's death. He moved into a homeless shelter right after Lara died. Within months, the director recognized Kip's computer skills. Reaching out to several companies, the pastor found a job opening, and when an offer came through, Kip accepted. The once homeless and despondent man began to rebuild his life piece by piece. The most significant part, his wife, was missing.

*Had I been living on the streets?* The loss seemed as fresh as yesterday and a lifetime ago. Walking life's path required soles of hope and resilience. *Otherwise, we just let go, and I'd come close.* He remembers his first day at the shelter and his last. Kip believed his story resembled Lazarus' resurrection from the dead.

\* \* \*

Kips walks through the park toward his office. A commotion is underway. It is the bench where he sat on that fateful day. An ambulance is waiting outside the fence. EMTs are placing a man on a gurney. *Gosh, and his dog, too?* Kip frowns. He glimpses the man's face just before they cover it. A pinch of sorrow holds him. *A good man,* h*e* thinks as he bids farewell.

The frail man's elbow peeks from under the sheet as his body lies on a dolly. Kip is seized by the reality that the man and his companion have died. He steps back and leans against a tree. The bark is coarse and thick, rubbing the back of his shirt. From the corner of his eye, a Latina woman, perhaps mid-forties, walks nearer to the bench. She keeps a respectful distance as the medics do their work. He understands why she is here.

The authorities try to keep gawkers at bay. Still, Kip catches another figure inching closer. A preteen boy is pulling a woman toward the bench. The woman appears confused, as if the child wants a better view of the macabre scene. Kip knows better. The boy wants this woman to have a turn. *It's his mom.*

Before Lara's death, Kip might have been proprietary over this bench and called these visitors interlopers.

But not today. He understands their desire to return to that incredible place. He's returned to this spot several times, hoping for a repeat experience, but none has been forthcoming. *If blessed once, you will never forget it.* Kip hopes to share the message he received through example.

\* \* \*

On the day his wife died, freezing rain pelted the earth. As a despondent Kip's life drained away, a stranger appeared and sat beside him on this bench. The man, of course, was an apparition- a being clothed in nothing more than a tunic and shower shoes. Yet the husband needed answers. "Why?" he asked the man with the kindest eyes he had ever seen.

\* \* \*

*Was he God? Brahma, Jesus, Buddha, or Mohammad?* Kip still isn't sure, but the visitor's identity is not as important as the message the specter shared. The warm breath entered his body. Pneuma. Kip understands this now. The Spirit breathes life into every human, creating a divine webbing, all a part of the Divine.

"Why did my wife have to die? Why do we suffer?"

Kip asked the stranger. His intonation was accusatory. His insides twisted like a wrung-out cloth.

"All mortals die. You are only a spirit passing through," the stranger's soft tone offered. Some will depart young, and others ancient. Sometimes, humans cause death, or it is time. It is all part of the journey and experience." His voice comforted him, like a parent, teacher, or friend.

"But Lara wasn't even forty years old. She had everything to live for. Why take her?" Kip raised the knuckle of his finger to his lips, stifling a sob of anguish.

"It's okay then for a fifty-year-old to die instead of your wife because that person had ten more years? Their families cry just as you do. Should the parents of a child who dies think Lara's death timely because she had forty years here? Life becomes judged by relativism. All life is sacred, Kip. The human construct of time does not measure contribution."

Kip sniffed. He studied the stranger's peaceful face. "It seems arbitrary to me. The idea of providence, some grand plan for all this, is far-fetched." The corners of his mouth drooped.

"Is it?" The stranger asked, perplexed. "Look around,

Kip. A divine proportion is in all of life—the Golden Ratio. Nothing, to the degree of this complexity, is created without a plan. We could not assemble a car from a vast heap of random junk." He laughed so hard that Kip joined in.

"I want to believe we'll be together again," Kips whispered.

"You will always be connected." The man pointed toward Kip's chest.

A brilliant light emanated from Kip's body, arcing across the sky.

"Do you understand?" The man's touch was gentle as he placed his hand on Kip and smiled.

"Memories give life to those who are departed."

"Like ghosts?" Kip's eyes widened.

"No. In the human mind," the man replied.

Kip scrutinized his hands. "Who are you?"

"The Great, I am. The Alpha and the Omega creating humankind in our image and likeness, knowing its imperfections. Humans experience the wonderful, powerful, messy, complicated, conditional, confounded thing called life. And when the journey ends, the love from which you come—returns to its Source."

"Sounds like a riddle." His anger reminded him of the events that brought him here. "What type of loving god would do this?" Kip gestured at his body. His tattered clothes, dirty face, and tangled beard. "Does a god take perverse pleasure in human misery? Are we nothing more than lab mice?" His voice cracked, giving sadness an opening.

"Does suffering have a purpose?" the being asked. It was a question.

"I haven't found it," Kip snapped, sounding like a six-year-old child, but he didn't care. *I want to let him have it.*

"What did you learn from Lara's journey? From your path?"

"Life sucks, and then you die." Kip huffed and crossed his arms.

The stranger's eyes pierced through Kip's armor of rage, finding the wreck of this man and lifting him.

"Life cannot be perfect, Kip. If it were, there would

be no purpose or meaning. You would move day to day without recognition or appreciation of it."

"Again, with those riddles." His tone was less acerbic. He sighed, peering into the stranger's eyes. "I'm sorry. I need to understand. Please."

"All humans experience a life with imperfections - some more tragic than others. Loss, pain, and tears of sadness are often brought by human hands, whether by accident, with malice, or because the mind is broken. But suffering has a purpose. It reminds humanity that this world is only temporary. Understanding the impermanence of this existence changes everything."

Kip interrupted. "Why do you let this happen? Humans didn't cause Lara's death. She had cancer. If life is hard enough, why allow us to harm each other? Where was this, *we,* during The Holocaust, or the Ukrainian, Cambodian, Armenian, and Rwandan Genocides? When the crazed slaughtered tens of millions of people?"

"We were there but did not cause humankind to kill or inflict injury. We do not sit on the side of sin or the sidelines. Holiness stands amidst it—surrounding the victims of such senseless, prideful cruelty. You may not have sensed our presence when your wife died, but Lara did. Those who are making their transition from this journey do. They see who they need to see. Their spouse, mother, father, child, Jesus, or other religious figures. We are here again to assure you are not alone in your suffering."

Kip wiped his eyes and straightened. "Lara felt you?"

The man nodded his head. "Your wife did not die alone. We were present, and your love flowed through her, and that is the mystic chord of memory that binds us."

The temperature dropped as they sat on the bench, filling the air with the diamond dust of tiny ice crystals. Yet the stranger kept Kip warm as he listened.

"Many humans are oblivious to the suffering of others. They are focused on their circumstances, unaware of the individual next to them on a bus ride, a coworker, a neighbor, or sometimes, a person in their home. It is easy to become self-absorbed and the victim—even when they are not the sufferer."

A flush crawled up Kip's neck. *I felt sorry for myself when Lara was dying.*

"When humankind suffers, we suffer—we are one. The whole body aches if you gash your leg." The stranger inhaled.

Kip dug his fingernails into his palms. "How do I go on?"

"You stand at a critical crossroads. Suffering remains senseless, and victimhood thrives. Or you find meaning, become aware of other's pain, and recognize the connection- oneness.

"The gash on the leg."

"Correct. Can you help lift someone else's agony? With action, not talk."

Kip was impervious to the arctic breeze that flowed past them.

The apparition continued. "Humanity thinks of love as perfection, the sappy sentiments in greeting cards getting it just right. But, like life, it isn't, and life experiences teach that things will be messy. The Divine doesn't ask for perfection. But we do not expect humans to pull so far away from their origin that they become unrecognizable, even to us. Humanity struggles to remember its true divine connection. They sleep under the illusion of separateness." He paused and pulled the sleeve of his tunic. His inner illumination seeps through the garment, like a luminous liquid transforming the fabric into a canvas of radiant light. "People see individual trees, not the complicated web of relationships, alliances, and kinship networks buried in their root system."

"Suffering is so hard. It's like a knife carving out the heart." Kip's eyes brimmed with the tears he thought were long gone.

The man took Kip's hand. "Maybe losing everything, including your wife, awakens that connection?" He tilted his head. Beneath the burlap robes, an inner glow grew brighter. Light oozed through his skin, running down his arms and out of his fingertips.

Kips said. "May I ask one more question?"

The stranger's hand had vaporized into a mist, releasing Kip's hand. Only a silhouette remained. "Please."

"I want to believe all this, but…"

"A Jewish word, meitzar. The narrow place where life is hard and having faith seems impossible. Pride lies and has you convinced you're on your own." He stopped. "Take a deep breath, Kip."

Kip inhaled, filling his lungs.

"Hold that breath for just a minute. Now describe the images."

Kip thought for a moment. "The mystic chords of memory, binding us through our shared experiences, history, emotions, and humanity. One giant matrix." He recognized the faces and their connections. The older man was at the VA when he returned from Iraq. The man, a World War II veteran, gave hugs and chatted with the soldiers. He also lost his wife and consoled Kip about Lara's illness. The Latina woman worked at the hospital where Lara spent her last days. She placed a small glass filled with lilies beside his wife's bed. The woman offered a prayer. Though now older, the preteen boy had once been a student in Lara's class.

"While imperceptible to the human eye, lives and narratives are intertwined. Just as humans seldom recognize their interconnectedness, faith is invisible. Like breathing, people don't give it much thought until they need it. Hope allows you to move beyond the cruelty of the world and all its hardships. To see life with more than physical eyes. Faith doesn't take away life's imperfections or suffering but gets you through them. Humanity has an innate longing for something greater than this world in which it exists. Faith is the reality of what we hope for, the proof of what we don't see." His voice faded, and the stranger vanished with a flash of light.

\* \* \*

"Night, Mr. Homestead," the junior assistant calls out as Kip leaves the office.

"Good night. See you in the morning, and thanks for your help today." Kip gave the young woman a slight salute. She beams at the acknowledgment. He thinks *it takes nothing to say a few kind words.*

He walks down the sidewalk, still hectic with workers leaving for the day. His stomach complains. Kip pops into a local restaurant, where he often gets a quick soup and sandwich for dinner. In a glass case, a giant chocolate chip cookie calls him. "I'll take one of those cookies, please." He pays and continues his walk toward the shelter.

"Hey, Kip," the pastor called out. "How have you been?"

"Great." He looks around, realizing every bed will be filled tonight despite the mild weather. More and more people have been showing up at the shelter for a meal, necessities, and, if fortunate, a place to sleep. Kip takes in the faces of the visitors and understands the word invisible. He walks through the facility, acknowledging people as he passes. When he arrives at a little girl's bed, he stops, reaches into the bag, and retrieves the morsel.

The girl's eyes widened, her smile exposing a gap in her front teeth. "Wow!" She gasped. "For me?" Her hand crosses over to cover the stump of her missing hand. She does not reach for the treat. At perhaps five years of age, she has learned not to assume anything or take things for granted.

"Indeed, my lady." Kip hands her the oversized cookie in a flourishing gesture and bows.

"Gee, thanks, Kip," the child says, breaking the wafer into four pieces with one hand. "Some kids would love a piece."

"That's very nice of you, Gwenivere. And how was your day?"

The girl is timid as she wraps each portion in a tissue. Her face flushes as she whispers, "Can I tell you a secret, Kip?"

His heart sinks to his feet. *Please don't let something have happened to her.* "Sure, I am all ears." His smile loses its vigor.

"You may not believe me," she says, twisting her mouth into a coy grin.

"Go ahead—try me," he responds, lifting a stray hair from her face.

"Well, today, Mom said to play in the park. I was watching the kids, and nobody asked me to play." She raises the stump of her missing hand. "So, I sat on a bench and… You'll never believe who sat next to me."

# Acknowledgments

Writing is a living, breathing art that doesn't end once your words have been put to page. Multiple iterations come forth from your mind, with the author tweaking this, editing that, or deleting all of the above.

Unlike other forms of artistry, where the creator applies the final brush stroke, fires it in the kiln, or glazes their work, writing requires a community. You rely on this community to give their time, thoughts, and reactions generously. And, of course, along the way, an edit or two or three (you get it).

Advanced readers are more than people willing to read your work and give feedback. They are your coach, critic, cheering section, and hand holders. They let you know when your work is ready to launch or needs more baking time. They read your work and come through when you need them most.

I have been blessed with multiple advanced readers (you know who you are) who are more than readers. To borrow a cliché, you are the wind beneath my wings. Thank you.

Printed in Dunstable, United Kingdom